The Freshwater Angler™

CATCHING PANFISH

Tactics for Sunfish, Crappies, Yellow Perch and White Bass

Shawn Perich

Creative Publishing
international
www.creativepub.com

An avid angler, Shawn Perich has fished for many species from coast to coast. He has written several books about fishing, including *Fly-Fishing the North Country* and *Superior Seasons*. His writings about the outdoors have appeared in numerous publications, including a long-running column in *Minnesota Outdoor News*. Shawn is also the publisher of *Northern Wilds,* a quarterly publication devoted to outdoor activities in the North Country. He lives in Hovland, Minnesota, on Lake Superior's North Shore.

Creative Publishing international

Copyright © 2006 by Creative Publishing international, Inc.
18705 Lake Drive East
Chanhassen, MN 55317
1-800-328-3895
www.creativepub.com

President/CEO: Ken Fund
Executive Editor: Barbara Harold
Creative Director: Brad Springer
Book Designer: Kari Johnston
Production Manager: Linda Halls

Printed in Singapore
10 9 8 7 6 5 4 3 2 1

CATCHING PANFISH
by Shawn Perich

Contributing Photographers: Mark Emery, Eric Engbretson, Bill Lindner, Tom Migdalski, Doug Stamm

Library of Congress Cataloging-in-Publication Data
Perich, Shawn.
  Catching panfish : tactics for sunfish, crappies, yellow perch and white bass / Shawn Perich.
     p. cm. -- (The freshwater angler series)
  Includes index.
ISBN-13: 978-1-58923-259-4
  ISBN-10: 1-58923-259-3 (hard cover)
  1. Panfish fishing. 2. Fly fishing. I. Title. II. Freshwater angler.
  SH691.P35P47 2006
  799.1'1--dc22   2005035042

TABLE OF CONTENTS

Introduction

Panfish are the common denominators of angling. Young anglers often get their start by fishing for sunfish or other panfish species that are readily accessible and easy to catch.

Although they may lack the glamour and allure of large game fish, panfish are hands-down fishing favorites. Abundant in most waters and good to eat, casual and expert anglers often target panfish. Across North America, anglers catch untold millions of panfish each year.

You don't need to invest a fortune in tackle or travel to exotic locales to be a successful panfish angler. Simple tackle and a nearby fishing hole will suffice. As you learn more about catching panfish, your techniques may become more sophisticated, but even novice anglers can land plenty of fish. After you have fun catching them, you can bring panfish home as the main component of a delicious dinner.

In this book, panfish include a variety of fish species. Some, like sunfish, are widely distributed; while you'll only find others, such as cisco, in certain regions. But no matter where you live, you'll find several of the species featured here in close-to-home waters.

This book provides what you need to know to find fishing places and catch fish throughout the year. A brief natural history informs you about the life cycles of the species.

Fishing for panfish is often seasonal in nature. You can learn about the best times to go fishing and where the fish are likely to be located in spring, summer, and fall. Ice fishing is enormously popular in the north, so this book includes a special section devoted to on-ice tactics for common panfish, as well as offbeat species like smelt.

If you are new to fishing, consider this book a stepping-stone to a lifetime of enjoyment. Presented in these pages are the basics of freshwater fishing, from using and keeping live bait to learning how to flyfish. The intent is to tickle your imagination and get you started—the only real way to learn about fishing is by spending time on the water. So go fish...and have fun!

Chapter 1
Equipment

Fishing for panfish can be as simple or as sophisticated as you want it to be. Generations of children have caught untold bluegills and other sunfish using whatever fishing tackle was available to them.

In parts of the U.S., the humble cane pole remains a popular tool for hoisting panfish from dense aquatic cover. However, an array of specially designed rods, reels, and terminal tackle is available to meet specific panfishing situations. In addition, flyfishing for panfish continues to gain popularity. Panfish tackle options are many, so you can choose an outfit that suits your needs and your pocketbook. As your fishing knowledge and experience grows, your tackle needs may expand for special methods and situations.

You may even decide that you need a boat or a float tube to reach new fishing holes. Buying a boat is a decision that requires forethought, because the craft must be suited to the waters where you use it and to your fishing style. You may also need marine electronics for on-the-water navigation and finding fish.

When selecting panfish tackle, consider the size and species of fish you'll target and typical fishing conditions you'll encounter. Generally, you can use lighter tackle than you would use to fish for bass, walleyes, or other freshwater game fish. Most popular panfish weigh about 1 pound (0.45 kg), so you don't need heavy line, large hooks, or big floats to catch them. In fact, novice anglers are often "over gunned" when they gear up for panfish. In most situations, "go light" is the best advice. Not only will you catch more fish, but you'll enjoy catching them more, too.

Boats

Marine manufacturers don't sell "bluegill boats," but many watercraft are suited to panfish fishing. A canoe or jon boat is all you need to fish on ponds, small lakes, and streams. It is best to fish large lakes and reservoirs with a standard fishing boat. Northern anglers generally prefer boats with deep V hulls for use on large, windy lakes. Southern anglers often choose flat-bottomed crafts that can negotiate shallow or weedy areas. Pontoon boats provide a large, stable platform where a family or other group of anglers can comfortably fish together.

You can outfit a fishing boat with all sorts of accoutrements to help you catch fish. Two items warrant special consideration. The first is an electric motor, which allows you to move your boat with minimal noise and disturbance, making it easier to approach skittish fish. The second is an electronic depth- or fish-finder. These units allow you to "see" fish beneath your boat. More importantly, they help you determine the depth, bottom composition, amount of submerged vegetation, and even water temperature of places you plan to fish. Knowing the habitat preferences of the species you seek will help you find fish.

Bluegill fishing is a simple pleasure even for experienced anglers.

Shore Fishing

In most regions, it is easy to find shore-fishing locations, especially during spring and early summer, when most species are spawning or feeding in the shallows. The dock at a lake cottage, public fishing area, or access site may be an excellent place to fish—especially if there is aquatic habitat within casting range. Sometimes, the dock itself may shelter bluegills or sunfish. Crappies and yellow perch may forage near the dock during low light periods. At any rate, a dock is a convenient angling platform and a great spot for kids to learn the basics of angling. You can find places to fish from shore by noticing where other folks are fishing. Often you will see bank anglers near bridges, in public parks, below dams, along public road right-of-ways, or on canals. Farm ponds are often stocked with panfish. When fishing private ponds or shorelines, be sure you have the landowner's permission.

Special tackle isn't necessary for shore fishing. However, in many situations a float helps you control your bait. A long fishing rod—7 feet (2.1 m) or more—makes it easier to cast greater distances. A pair of hip boots or chest waders lets you wade through shallow water or marsh vegetation to reach deeper water. Growing numbers of anglers use float tubes or inflatable pontoon crafts to get away from the bank, gaining the mobility of a boat or canoe without the expense.

Many anglers begin their fishing careers casting for panfish from a dock.

Electronics

Many anglers rely on electronics to find fish, mark good fishing spots, and even identify the species of fish swimming beneath them. Depth finders, Global Positioning Units (GPS), and underwater cameras have made it possible for anglers to learn many of the secrets that lie beneath the water's surface and catch more fish. You can spend a small fortune on top-of-the-line electronics, though for most panfish anglers, a modest investment will suffice.

Nearly every fishing boat is equipped with a depth finder, a sonar device that shows the depth and often fish swimming beneath the boat on an onboard display. Depth finders are invaluable in aiding navigation and for finding underwater structure and fish. Many models include a surface-water temperature sensor and measure the speed at which your boat is moving. Knowing water temperature is often important to locating fish in the spring or anytime fish are concentrated where they find their preferred water temperature. You can use the speed indicator to keep a consistent speed when trolling.

GPS allows anglers to mark the exact location of a spawning bed, a productive piece of structure, or even the launch ramp. Many anglers share GPS coordinates of productive fishing areas. You can store coordinates in the memory of your GPS unit. GPS is invaluable for safely navigating in fog or adverse conditions.

Underwater cameras have become a standard tool for many ice anglers, because anglers can watch for approac-hing fish. Open-water anglers use them to scout new locations, learn more about the makeup of the lake bottom, and identify fish they mark on their depth finder.

Using ultralight spinning gear allows you to cast tiny panfish baits.

Rods and Reels

Rods and reels suitable for panfish range from inexpensive spin-cast and spinning outfits to extra-long poles designed for crappie and bluegill fishing. The most important consideration when selecting a panfish outfit is to pick one that it is suited to the line you intend to use. Generally, this means you want a rod-and-reel combination labeled light or ultralight.

Another consideration is your skill level as an angler. Spin-cast reels, with which you push a button to release the line when making a cast, are an excellent choice for children and novices. Spinning reels are most common and many anglers prefer them, though novices may need some practice to become proficient at using them. Bait-casting reels require even more practice and anglers generally use them with heavier lines and terminal tackle.

Choosing a fishing rod is partly about function and partly a matter of personal taste. A rod must match the reel you intend to use with it, both in style (a spin-cast rod for a spin-cast reel) and in balance—you can't put a big-game reel on an ultralight rod.

Nearly all rods from major manufacturers have information on the shaft regarding the action and the recommended line weight. Most manufacturers rate rods suitable for panfish as ultralight, light, or medium actions. Use ultralight rods to cast very small baits or lures, which are often effective for panfish. Use light- or medium-action rods with somewhat heavier baits—these are a good choice if you intend to fish for other species in addition to panfish.

Standard rod lengths range from 5 to 8 feet (1.5 to 2.4 m). The longer rods make it easier to cast greater distances and to control your line. Anglers use 9- to 16-foot "poles" (2.7- to 4.9-m) to dangle baits amid dense brush or vegetation.

Line

Manufacturers provide today's angler with a wide selection of monofilament, cofilament, and braided lines. Choosing the right line can be a difficult decision if you are unfamiliar with the characteristics of the various products.

For common spinning and spin-cast tackle, a quality monofilament line from 2- to 6-pound-test (0.9- to 2.7-kg) is adequate. The light line is less visible to the fish and allows small baits and lures to have life-like action. Very light lines, such as 2-pound-test, break easily, so they are not the best choice for young or inexperienced anglers. Six-pound-test is more forgiving, so you can pull loose from snags or tangles in vegetation.

Monofilament more than 8-pound-test (3.6-kg) is too heavy for anything but specialized situations, such as where you must hoist your catch out of brush or mats of aquatic vegetation.

You can use braided lines, which have significantly thinner diameter than monofilament, in some situations where you'll need a strong line. However, braids are more visible to fish, so you may need a monofilament leader.

Fluorocarbon is a monofilament that combines strength with near invisibility underwater. Fluorocarbon is often used as a leader material.

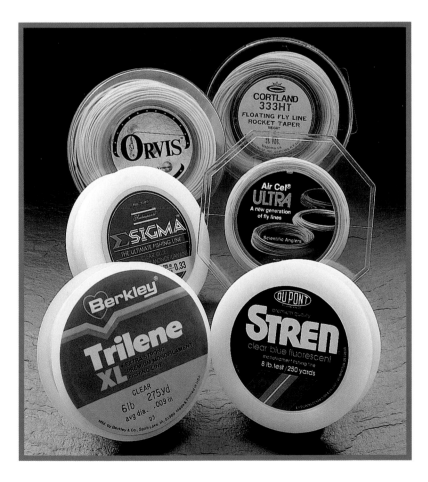

Whatever your brand you will find high-grade fly line is more durable and easier to cast than inexpensive line.

Hook size depends on the size of the fish's mouth. Use hooks as large as 2/0 for crappies and as small as #10 for sunfish.

Shank length is a matter of personal preference. Many anglers prefer long-shank hooks because they are easiest to remove.

Terminal Tackle

At one end of a fishing line sits an angler. On the other end is a hook and sinker—terminal tackle. This "business end" of a fishing line is what catches the fish, so the selection of proper terminal tackle is important. Sometimes, anglers assume that because panfish are easy to catch, they don't need to be fussy about tackle selection. You can spend a lifetime acquiring tackle—and most anglers do—but when you are on the water, having the tackle suited to your fishing situation often means the difference between catching fish and going home skunked.

Hooks

Choose hooks matched to your bait and that are small enough to easily fit inside a fish's mouth when it bites. A wide range of hook styles are available.

Some anglers like long-shanked hooks, because they are easiest to remove from the fish. You can pull a bendable light-wire hook out of most snags. Also, light-wire hooks are best for fishing with delicate baits, such as crickets.

In some bait-fishing situations, anglers prefer circle hooks, because the design hooks a fish in the corner of the mouth, rather than the fish swallowing the bait.

Colored hooks, which are generally red or another bright color, give some added attraction to your presentation.

Be sure your hooks are sharp. New, high quality hooks are very sharp. Carry a hook hone in your tackle box to sharpen hooks while you are fishing.

Sinkers

Sinkers deliver your bait to the depth where fish are feeding. Using too much or too little weight may affect your fishing success.

Split shot are the most common sinkers and are applicable for fishing with or without floats.

Slip sinkers slide along your fishing line, so the fish doesn't feel the weight when it takes the bait. Popular slip sinker styles include eggs, bullets, and walking sinkers.

Lead has long been the standard material for making sinkers. Due to environmental concerns associated with lead, manufacturers also offer sinkers made from other materials.

Floats

Floats, often called bobbers, present a suspended bait. The first fishing experience for many anglers is fishing for sunfish with a bobber. The visual aspect of float fishing—the float goes underwater when a fish takes the bait—makes it easy for novices to learn the rudiments of fishing. Float fishing is an effective way to catch panfish in many situations. Some anglers have adapted

Select a float that slides easily, such as a tube or cylinder float. Or use a clip-on bobber set so the clip rests on the plastic (left to right, left).

Attach a bobber stop at the depth you want to fish. You can buy a commercial type or simply tie a piece of rubber band to the line (below left).

Thread on a small bead, then the float. Tie on a hook, then add enough split-shot for balance about 8 inches up the line (below).

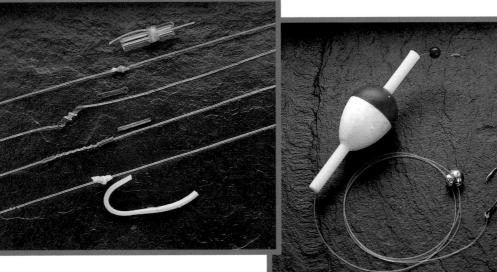

European floats and fishing techniques to North American panfish waters for refined, light-tackle presentations.

You can divide floats into two basic categories: fixed and sliding. A fixed float attaches to the line, usually with a spring-tension clip or another knotless method. Fixed floats are best suited to depths of less than 6 feet (1.8 m).

A sliding float slips freely along the line and holds at the proper depth with a small rubber or knot stop. With a sliding float, you can fish at greater depths, because you can reel up the stop and the float slips down to the terminal tackle when you make a cast. Usually, manufacturers paint floats in bright colors for better visibility.

It is important to match the size of the float to the size of the fish you intend to catch. A 7-inch (18-cm) bluegill can't submerge a tennis-ball-sized bobber intended for northern pike. When a fish takes your bait, it should be able to pull your float under with minimal resistance. An elongated float offers better floatation and less resistance than a round bobber.

You can add weight to your line or the float to reduce buoyancy. Adding weight to floats helps to achieve neutral buoyancy and improve casting performance.

Some floats contain tiny lights for night fishing. A variety of float styles allow you to fine-tune your presentation in wavy conditions, current, or to fool wary fish. You can even find popper floats that gurgle, pop, and rattle when you pull them across surface. The commotion may attract fish.

Fly Fishing

Fly fishing for panfish is increasingly popular, especially when the fish are in relatively shallow water to spawn or feed. It is easy and inexpensive to get started in fly fishing, and panfish are excellent quarry for beginners. All you need is a fly rod and reel, and a basic selection of flies. With a little practice, you can easily learn basic flycasting.

In most situations, if you can cast well enough to accurately place a fly 30 to 40 feet (9.1 to 12.2 m) away, you can catch panfish. Generally, panfish are less finicky and selective than fish such as trout, so a simple selection of flies and poppers are all you need to begin fly fishing.

The most important aspect of selecting a fly-fishing outfit is matching the rod to the weight of the fly line. Manufacturers use a number system, ranging from 2 (lightest) to 12 (heaviest), to indicate the line weight. Weights 4 through 7

are suitable for panfish.

Fly lines come in floating and sinking styles, as well as in different tapers to meet varied casting needs. A good, entry-level selection for is a floating, weight-forward line.

Many anglers consider a 6-weight outfit a good choice for all-around fly fishing. Match the line with a fly rod 8 to 9 feet (2.4 to 2.7 m) in length.

You don't need to spend a fortune on a fly rod, but it is a good idea to select a model from a manufacturer that specializes in fly fishing. Since the reel's primary function is to store the line, an inexpensive, single-action fly reel is adequate to complete the outfit. Attach a 6- to 12-foot (1.8- to 3.6-m) tapered leader to the end of your fly line. The leader tippet can be anywhere from 6- to 2-pound-test (2.7- to 0.9-kg).

The mechanics of fly casting differ from spin- or bait-casting, because you cast the weight of the fly line rather than the weight of the bait or lure. In fly-casting, timing is everything. Most beginners

make the mistake of rushing their casting motions. Instead, make sure the line completes its arc and "loads" the rod before you continue the cast. Turn your head to watch the back cast unfurl and then make the forward cast. Practice casting on your lawn, a pond in the local park, or a similar location to lessen frustration when you go fishing. Also learn the roll cast, which allows you to fish in locations where there is no room for a back cast.

While trout anglers often talk about "matching the hatch"—imitating a specific insect that the fish are eating—panfish anglers often use general, attractor flies. Panfish patterns include standard wet flies and nymphs, such as the Coachman or Wooly Worm, floating foam bugs, and cork or balsa poppers. Carry a selection of dark, bright, and subdued colors.

Fishing on the surface with bugs and poppers is enjoyable, but subsurface fishing with wet flies may be more productive. Keep trying different patterns until you have success.

Matching Rod and Line Weight to Fly Size

Rod/Line Weight	Fly Size Range	Rod/Line Weight	Fly Size Range
3	28 – 12	6	20 – 6
4	26 – 10	7	16 – 4
5	24 – 8	8	12 – 1/0

Consider the size of the flies you'll be using when choosing a fly rod. As a rule, the heavier your rod and line weight, the larger the fly you can comfortably and effectively cast.

Flies for sunfish

include: (1) poppers, such as the Pan Pop; (2) sponge bugs, such as the Creepy Cricket; (3) nymphs, such as the Hare's Ear; (4) wet flies, such as the Wooly Worm; and (5) dry flies, such as the Black Gnat.

Use a popper with a nymph dropper to catch sunfish in shallow water. The popper will attract the aggressive fish and the nymph will catch the neutral fish.

Chapter 2

Live Bait

Lift a rock, then check for nymphs or larvae on the underside. This is a good way to collect caddis cases, stone-fly nymphs and other insect larvae.

Y ou can catch all panfish species on some form of live bait. Fishing with bait is consistently effective throughout the year. Most bait-fishing techniques are simple and easy to learn, which makes them excellent for introducing children and novices to fishing.

The only drawbacks to using live bait are that you could find it difficult to acquire, you must keep it alive while you are fishing, and you may find it messy to use. However, the ready availability of packaged bait and its fish-catching advantages nearly always outweigh the drawbacks.

The live bait industry is surprisingly large. Wholesalers and distributors may transport some baits from other states or even other countries. Other bait supplies are local or regional in nature and may only be seasonally available. At busy times of year, bait may be in short supply. Well-informed anglers may buy bait in advance of a planned fishing excursion or in large quantities so they have it when they need it. Fishing shops can help you select the best bait for a particular fishing situation.

Always check bait before you buy it to ensure it is fresh and lively. Proper care and storage when you are fishing will keep it that way.

Trapping (above) is the most common method because it is the simplest and causes the least amount of damage to the baitfish.

Seining (right) is a little more difficult than trapping because it requires two people, in most cases, and waders. One pass, however, with a seining net could yield enough baitfish for a whole weekend of fishing.

Worms

Worms are a reliable bait for most panfish species. Anglers commonly use several varieties of earthworms. They vary is size from 2 inches (5 cm) to more than 6 inches (15.2 cm) in length. You can collect your own worms, buy them at a bait shop, or even purchase them from mail-order suppliers.

Nightcrawlers are the largest fishing worms. You can collect them after dark when they emerge from their burrows and lie on the surface of the ground. Walk quietly over a mowed lawn and shine a light on the ground. When you see a nightcrawler, slowly reach down, and grasp it firmly by the head. Because nightcrawlers often keep their tails in the burrow, they can quickly withdraw and get away.

You may need to pull with steady pressure to get a worm out of its burrow. The best time to collect nightcrawlers is in the spring or after a rain, when they emerge from the saturated soil.

Store nightcrawlers in commercial bedding, moist moss (not saturated), or soil. Feed nightcrawlers used coffee grounds (be sure they are cool) or kitchen compost. Keep your worm container in a cool, dark place, such as your basement or a refrigerator.

Because nightcrawlers are so large, you can break them and use part of the worm for bait. Always use the tail piece first, because the worm will regenerate a new tail. How do you tell the head from the tail on a nightcrawler? The head of the nightcrawler is darker than the tail. The head also has a ring called the collar, which is used during reproduction.

Red wigglers and red worms are smaller worms (average size, 2 inches/5 cm) that are commercially raised and widely available at bait shops. Also called manure worms, they are the best size to use for sunfish and other smaller panfish. Other commercially grown worms that are regionally available are gray nightcrawlers and African nightcrawlers. Both grow to about half the size of the common nightcrawler.

Backyard bait collectors can dig common garden worms, also called angler worms, in rich, moist soils. A small compost pit can provide the average angler with an endless supply. In the Southeast, anglers gather grunt worms from acidic soils, such as those found in pine forests.

Nightcrawlers should be kept cool and moist. Store them in commercial bedding, soil, or damp moss.

Leeches

Leeches are not for everyone. Squeamish anglers don't like to handle the slippery, slithering creatures. Some mistakenly assume the sucker-like mouth can fasten to their skin. In truth, the ribbon leech commonly used for bait does not feed on living flesh or blood.

Medicine leeches and horse leeches (which are bloodsuckers), are not as lively and much less effective as bait. You'll find bait leeches at retail outlets in small, medium, and jumbo sizes. In some areas, a smaller, livelier variety called the tiger leech is available and preferred for panfish.

Leeches are primarily sold in northern tier states and Canada, where they are a popular bait for walleyes. They make excellent bait for black crappies, yellow perch, and other panfish, too. Keep leeches in clean, cool water.

Leeches are a favorite panfish bait in northern states.

Aquatic Insects

Rocks, logs, and other debris submerged in lakes and streams can provide an ever-fresh supply of live bait. The nymphal stages of several insects are relatively easy to catch and large enough to bait a hook. Better still, they are a familiar food source to the fish that occupy the same waters.

If you use insects for bait, it is important to know what time of year you are most likely to find them. Some species are most numerous in spring and summer, before the nymphs become adult insects. Anglers use various "bugs," which go by a variety of local names, though the nymphs are members of several insect families.

Stoneflies, dragonflies, and dobsonflies live their aquatic lives as fierce-looking nymphs with hard, segmented bodies. Mayfly nymphs are more delicate and can be difficult to thread on a hook. Caddis flies live in cases made of tiny pebbles and vegetative debris that adhere to submerged rocks.

Collecting aquatic insects can be more challenging than fishing. Some quickly scuttle away when you turn over a rock. In moving water, you can use a screen or fine-mesh net to collect insects tumbling in the current as you turn over rocks or debris.

Almost every body of water provides a freshwater habitat for some type of insect life. Aquatic insects spend the early stages of their lives in the water and move to the surface to become adults.

Popular aquatic insects (above) include: (1) stonefly nymphs, (2) hellgrammites, (3) mayfly nymphs, (4) caddis pupae, and (5) waterworms.

Insects are a very important food source for many fish species (left).

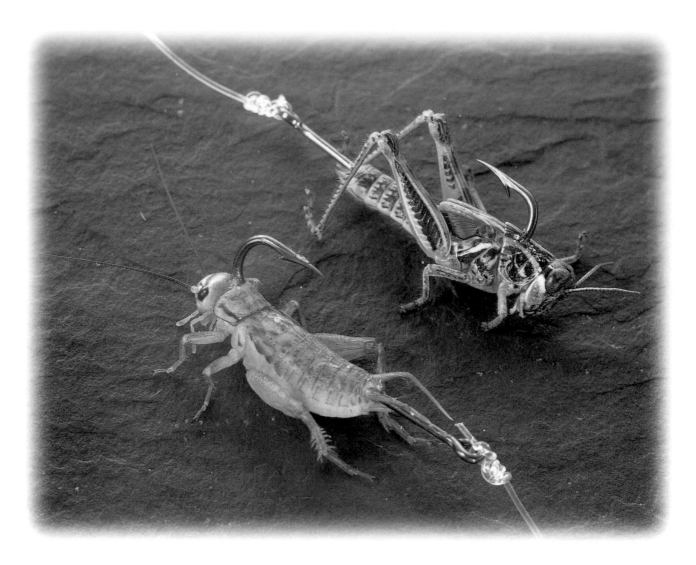

Thread crickets and grasshoppers on long-shank, light-wire hooks. The point should protrude between the collar and head, or pierce the collar.

Crickets and Grasshoppers

In some locales, crickets are a favorite bait for sunfish. They may be available at bait shops or pet supply stores. If they're available, you'll hear them as you step through the door. Grasshoppers are abundant during the summer and early fall.

The wind often blows grasshoppers into the water on breezy days and they are a favored food for many fish species. You can easily catch and collect grasshoppers for bait. The best time to seek them is early in the morning when there is dew on the grass, because they are sluggish before the sun warms them. Store the grasshoppers and crickets in a cage or container that allows you to take one out without the rest escaping.

Larvae

Waxworms, mealworms, mousies, spikes, and maggots are among the larvae commonly used as bait. They are especially popular for ice-fishing. Various larvae are seasonally available at bait shops. To ensure freshness, always open the container and inspect the bait before you purchase it. Store larvae in a cooler or refrigerator to keep them alive and prevent the larvae from turning into an adult insect.

Minnows

Live minnows are excellent bait for crappies, yellow perch, and white bass, and at times are effective for most panfish species. Generally, panfish anglers use the smallest minnows (sometimes called crappie minnows) available. Some anglers capture their own minnows using traps, seines, or throw nets. Depending on the weather, minnows will remain alive for a few hours in a bucket of water with minimal care. Minnows keep best in cool, aerated water. Some minnow species are hardier than others. Often a bait dealer can tell you what species will best suit your fishing needs.

Common Shiner

Creek Chub

Gizzard Shad

White Sucker

Golden Shiner

Cisco

When Is the Best Time To Go Fishing?

An old adage contends that the best time to go fishing is whenever you have the opportunity. Most anglers would agree with this wise advice. However, just because you go fishing whenever you can doesn't mean you'll always catch fish.

Knowing the best times to go fishing often makes the difference between a successful and a so-so outing. Although it is impossible to predict if the fish will bite, being on the water when they are most likely to bite tips the odds in your favor.

Inexperienced anglers may go fishing when it is most convenient and comfortable—like in the middle of the day. When the fish are especially active, such as during the spawning season, midday may be good fishing. Most of the time, though, fish retreat to deeper water and feed less actively at midday.

A good rule of thumb is to be on the water when the sun is low in the sky and sunlight isn't penetrating the water. Nearly all fish species feed actively during the low-light periods of early morning and late evening. For the same reason, fishing is often better on overcast days.

It is important to head to a hotspot when it is hot. Even famous fishing holes have their slow times. For instance, you may hear that a certain lake has good fishing for crappies. However, that reputation may rest on the excellent fishing that occurs during the April spawn. If you fish the lake during the August dog days, you may find the water is as warm and green as pea soup—and the famed crappies nowhere to be found. Talk to other anglers, fisheries managers, and bait shop staff to learn as much as you can about prime fishing times.

Weather can waylay the best-laid fishing plans. The arrival of a high-pressure cold front often puts a chill on the fishing. Most anglers prefer to fish when the barometer is falling or when the weather is stable. Wind or rain can make for uncomfortable, but productive fishing.

Get off the water when you hear thunder or see lightning, even in the distance.

Some anglers pay close attention to phases of the moon and Solunar Tables. Others monitor water temperatures, especially in spring and fall, watching for the optimal temperatures for spawning or feeding activity. Some go out when other anglers report they've had good fishing.

None of these strategies is foolproof, but all are likely to increase your chances of catching fish. Then again, most of us have constraints and responsibilities that limit our time on the water.

Since any fishing is better than no fishing, the best time to go fishing is when you have the opportunity to do so. It is difficult to argue with the wisdom of that time-honored advice!

Overcast days offer great fishing opportunities, from boat (above) as well as from shore (left). Fishing is usually best when the sun is low and less light penetrates the water.

Chapter 3
Sunfish

The name sunfish refers to the bright, sunny colors of these scrappy fighters. Some anglers refer to them as bream or brim. The sunfish family includes many species. They have many things in common, plus some features and behaviors that help distinguish each one from its relatives.

Bluegills

Mom, apple pie, and bluegills—no species can be better described as the all-American fish. Widely distributed across the United States, the bluegill is readily accessible to millions of anglers. In the South, anglers call bluegills bream. Often a cooperative quarry from shore, dock, or boat, the bluegill is an entry-level fish well suited to young or novice anglers. However, the species remains popular with anglers of all skill levels—a testament to its excellent flavor on the plate. The fact that bluegills are just plain fun to catch is a point in their favor, too!

Native to the eastern half of the country, stocking programs expanded the range of bluegills across the nation. Although they can tolerate and even thrive in a variety of water conditions, their preferred habitat is clear waters with moderate aquatic vegetation.

In streams, you'll most likely find bluegills in quiet areas away from the current. They can also survive in slightly brackish water. Although bluegills appear in all northern states, they prefer warmer water.

Bluegills have a subtle beauty. Though their saucer-shaped bodies are generally a mottled greenish-brown color, they have exquisite, light-blue gill covers that end with a black ear flap.

Males have a bright, burnt-orange breast, while females have yellow breasts. The colors are brightest during the spawn.

In some locales, bluegills have darker, vertical bars along their flanks, though they are less pronounced in larger fish. An identifying mark shared by all bluegills is a dark blotch at the rear base of the dorsal fin, not found on other sunfish.

Most anglers consider bluegills greater than 6 inches (15.2 cm) in length keepers. It is unusual for bluegills to exceed 10 inches (25.4 cm) in length or weigh more than 1 pound (0.5 kg). They are most likely to reach exceptional sizes in regions with optimal habitat and climate conditions, as well

as light fishing pressure. The world record bluegill weighed 4 pounds, 12 ounces (2.15 kg) and was caught in Alabama's Ketona Lake in 1950.

The diet of bluegills includes insects, tiny crustaceans, and small fish. Preferences vary based on the season, the aquatic ecosystem, and what's available. Bluegills will feed on aquatic vegetation when other foods are scarce. They will also eat tiny, aquatic organisms suspended in the water column called plankton. Bluegills will move within a body of water in order to find food.

In most water bodies, bluegills are about midway in the food chain, a link between small organisms and large predators. One common bluegill predator is the largemouth bass. Since predation helps keep prolific bluegill populations in balance within their niche in the ecosystem, a lake with a healthy bass population often provides good bluegill fishing.

■ Redear Range

Redear Sunfish

Throughout the South, the redear sunfish is a favorite among panfish anglers. Known as the shellcracker, because it has special teeth in the back of its throat to grind up snail shells, the redear grows somewhat larger than bluegills do. The world record redear, caught in a South Carolina diversion canal in 1998, weighed a whopping 5 pounds, 7.5 ounces (2.47 kg). Although its native range extends as far north as Iowa, the redear stocking programs introduced redear to waters in the western United States.

As the name shellcracker suggests, this sunfish feeds extensively on snails. A bottom feeder, the redear also eats other invertebrates and small fish. On occasion, they feed on or near the surface. They become less active in cool water and are unlikely to feed when water temperatures drop below 45°F (7.2°C).

Common in large lakes and reservoirs within their range, redear prefer clear water and areas with submerged vegetation. Favored habitat includes shady areas around stumps, fallen trees, and similar cover. During the summer, redear retreat to the depths and you might catch them in water 25 to 35 feet (7.6 to 10.7 m) deep. Redear may inhabit small lakes, ponds, and slow-moving streams and can tolerate brackish water.

You can easily identify shellcrackers by their orange-red edge along a dark ear-flap and yellow breast. They lack distinctive body markings and are light green to gold in color. Because they produce few young and are less likely to become over-abundant and stunted, redear have a larger average size than other sunfish. In good habitat, expect to catch shellcrackers ranging from 7 to 10 inches (17.8 to 25.4 cm) in length.

■ Pumpkinseed Range

Pumpkinseed

The pumpkinseed is proof that good things come in small packages. Few freshwater fish are as colorful or as easy to catch. Pumpkinseeds are an excellent entry-level fish for young or beginning anglers. Sometimes called common sunfish, they are native to the Midwest and East, but have been introduced elsewhere.

They prefer somewhat cooler water than other sunfish and do not live in brackish water. Inhabiting small lakes and ponds, slow-moving streams, and sheltered bays on larger lakes, they stay close to shore and in or near dense vegetation.

Adults are usually 5 to 7 inches (12.7 to 17.8 cm) long and weigh less than 1 pound (0.5 kg). The world record was caught from the North Saluda River in South Carolina in 1997 and weighed 2 pounds, 4 ounces (1.02 kg).

Bright coloration makes pumpkinseeds easily to identify. They are mostly gold along their flanks with speckled orange, green, and red markings. Iridescent blue highlights the face, gill covers, and edges of dorsal fin and tail. The dark ear flap has a bright red spot at the tip. The belly of a pumpkinseed ranges from bright yellow-orange to bronze. Coloration is the same in both sexes, but the males are more vivid.

Pumpkinseeds spawn in the spring at the same time and in the same manner as bluegills. Schools of fish build saucer-shaped nests in the same vicinity, where one or more females will deposit their eggs. The young hatch within one or two weeks, depending upon water temperature.

Pumpkinseeds grow slowly—less than 1 to 3 inches (less than 2.5 to 7.6 cm) the first year. Often it takes three years for them to reach a length of 4 inches (10.2 cm) and six years to grow to 6 inches (15.2 cm). Spawning adults in stunted populations may be less than 3 inches (7.6 cm) long. These diminutive fish feed on insects, mollusks, and small fish, including their own young.

Redbreast

Redbreast sunfish are common on the Atlantic Seaboard and now inhabit many southern waters. Also known as yellow-belly sunfish, you'll find this medium-sized member of the sunfish clan in both streams and still water. Redbreast can also tolerate slightly brackish conditions. It is most abundant in rivers within its native range.

Named for its bright, sunset-orange or yellow breast, this sunfish has a distinctive, long ear flap. An adult redbreast averages 6 inches (15.2 cm) in length and just a few ounces in weight, but the world record was a 2 pound, 1 ounce (0.93 kg) fish taken in Florida's Suwannee River in 1988.

Redbreasts build their spawning nests when the spring water temperature is about 68°F (20.0°C). Like pumpkinseeds, they are slow growing, feeding on insects, small fish, and other aquatic life.

In the fall, they gather in large schools in deep water. Their activity level slows to a state of near-hibernation throughout the winter. They are most active during and after the spring spawn.

■ Redbreast Range

Warmouth

The warmouth is a resident of backwaters, sloughs, and swamps found throughout the South and as far north as southern Minnesota. You can now also fish for warmouth in western states.

Known as the stumpknocker or goggle-eye perch, this fish has the ability to tolerate stagnant and turbid water conditions. It also tolerates somewhat brackish water.

Sometimes confused with the rock bass, which it resembles in coloration, the warmouth has only three spines on its anal fin, compared to six on the rock bass.

It may take a warmouth seven years to grow to 8 inches (20.3 cm). Florida's Yellow River produced the world record in 1985 weighing 2 pounds, 7 ounces (1.1 kg).

Warmouth eat crayfish, aquatic insect larvae, and small fish. Most of the feeding occurs early in the morning and nearly ceases in the afternoon.

You'll usually find warmouth in or around heavy cover in shallow water. Depending upon the locale, they spawn from spring throughout the summer. They have lower reproductive rates than most panfish, which helps prevent overpopulation.

Aside from incidental catches, they generally attract little attention from anglers.

Green Sunfish

The green sunfish is small, but hardy. It can live in waters that are inhospitable (including siltation, shifting water temperatures, and low oxygen levels) for other sunfish. You'll find green sunfish in waters ranging from the bayous of Louisiana to cold lake-trout waters on the Canadian border.

Although anglers do not often pursue these sunfish, you'll find them near the shore—around rocks, vegetation, or fallen trees. They are most active at dawn and dusk.

Most often, anglers consider the adults too small to keep. Two fish weighing 2 pounds, 2 ounces (0.96 kg) tie for the word record, one caught in 1971 from a Missouri reservoir and the other taken from a Kansas flooded mine pit in 1961.

Although they resemble a bass in body shape, they have all of the spawning and feeding characteristics of bluegills.

Longear Sunfish

The longear sunfish is a palette of bright colors, most notably orange and blue. Its namesake ear flap is exceptionally long and has a narrow, scarlet border.

Found from the Upper Midwest east to the upper St. Lawrence River and south to the Gulf Coast, the longear dwells in the quiet water of clear streams as well as in ponds and bogs.

One of the smallest sunfish, it takes five years for a longear to reach 4 inches (10.2 cm) in the North. Though it grows somewhat larger in southern climates, anglers consider a 6-inch (15.2-cm) large. The world record came from Elephant Butte Lake in New Mexico in 1985 and weighed 1 pound, 12 ounces (0.79 kg).

■ Longear Sunfish Range

Where to Find Sunfish

If you were to ask an average angler where to catch sunfish, the answer would likely be, "Off the end of the dock." Sunfish are so common that anglers often take them for granted. Schools of small ones are often visible from shore or beneath docks. However, larger sunfish, the size you want to bring home for dinner, are not necessarily so easy to find. They move about in lakes and reservoirs in response to water temperature, food availability, weather conditions, and, most importantly, changing seasons.

In early spring, just after ice-out in the North and prior to warming water temperatures in the South, you may find sunfish in shallow, mud-bottom bays, which are the first locations on a lake to begin warming up, spurring the growth of vegetation and aquatic insect activity. You may also find them in deeper water near spawning sites. When the spawn starts, sunfish move into the shallows during warm days and then retreat when the air and water temperatures cool in late afternoon.

Once spawning begins in earnest, sunfish are easy to locate if you can recognize spawning habitat. Look for shallow, protected bays and shorelines with a sand or gravel bottom and some aquatic vegetation. Often you can see the nest depressions, which are a different color than the lake bottom. Spawning sunfish avoid muddy water or areas with current. They prefer locations with sunny exposure. Continue checking spawning sites after activity peaks for late spawners, as well as males that stay behind to guard the nests.

After spawning, sunfish begin moving toward deeper water, where they spend the summer. While small sunfish populate the shallows, larger adults hold off the deep edge of the vegetation line. Look for them along the edge or in adjacent deep water.

During the summer, you will often find the biggest sunfish at depths of 20 to 30 feet (6.1 to 9.1 m). Though they spend most of their time near the bottom, sunfish will suspend to feed on plankton or insects. You may find sunfish near deep docks, fish cribs, or other man-made structure. Natural points, humps, and depressions in flats will hold fish. Gradual breaks are generally better than steep drop-offs.

In reservoirs, look for sunfish along channel edges, near the mouths of coves and creek arms, and around sunken islands or structure.

Expect sunfish to move into shallower areas during the low-light periods of early morning and evening. When sunlight penetrates the water, they'll go deeper and be less active. You may also find them in shady cover. Abrupt changes in weather, such as the arrival of a cold front, also slows fish activity.

In early fall, sunfish return to the deep breaks near their spring spawning areas. Generally, they won't go into the shallows where they spawn except for feeding forays on warm days. When the water temperature drops below 60°F (15.6°C), the fish migrate to deep-water wintering areas. Though ice-anglers pursue wintering sunfish in the North, few southern anglers fish for them.

Stump fields in shallow water provide extra cover. A stump protects one side of the nest, making it easier for the male to guard the young.

Move slowly along the edge of emergent weeds, while casting toward the vegetation (above). Or fan-cast a potential spawning area to locate fish.

A successful day of fishing (left) proves that a dock can be a good place to begin.

Add natural bait to an artificial to make the lure more appealing. Sunfish will hold the lure an instant longer before spitting it out.

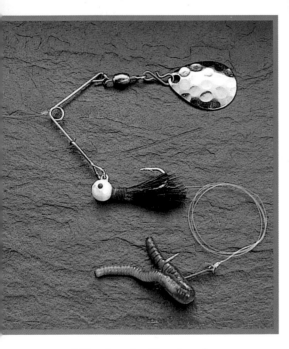

Attach a trailer hook with live bait behind an artificial lure, such as a small spinnerbait. The lure attracts sunfish to the bait.

Fishing Tactics

As everyone knows, catching sunfish is easy. Abundant in many waters, small sunfish populate the shallows where they are accessible to anglers. However, their larger kin are not necessarily so easy to locate.

Solitary fish may be scattered along a deep vegetation line or similar cover. Aside from the spawning season, don't expect to find big sunfish concentrated in large schools. Also, don't expect them to be eager biters. Often, they will slowly approach the bait, inspect it, and then back away. When they do bite, they inhale the bait—but they can exhale it just as quickly if they feel weight or the hook. Catching such finicky fish requires some finesse.

Use light line and small hooks to make the best natural presentations. In most situations, 6-pound-test (2.7-kg) monofilament is sufficient, though 4-pound (1.8 kg) or even 2-pound (0.9 kg) line may tip the odds in your favor when the water is clear or the fish are reluctant to bite.

Some anglers say that if sunfish grew to 10 pounds (4.5 kg), we still wouldn't know what they looked like, because they are such scrappers. Shaped like a plate, sunfish put up a lot of resistance when they turn perpendicular to the angler. Although they don't tail-walk across the water's surface or make long, sizzling runs, sunfish are determined fighters. Light tackle allows you to enjoy the battle.

Ultralight spinning tackle is the best choice to match with light lines and makes it easier to cast tiny baits and lures. In heavy cover, particularly in the South, anglers may use heavy line so they can pull free from snags.

If you use a hook that is too big, a sunfish may not be able to take the bait in its tiny mouth. For most baits, a #8 or #10 hook will suffice, though a #12 or even a miniscule #14 may be necessary for very small or fragile baits. When using small hooks, be aware the sunfish may swallow the bait, so keep a pair of pliers or a hook remover handy. Light-wire, long-shanked bait hooks are easier to remove, though they are less effective when the fish is hesitant to take bait.

Most anglers use bait when fishing for sunfish. In addition to a range of natural baits, a number of commercial products have the scent and texture intended to attract sunfish. Bait is the best choice when the water is cold and the fish are less active. Bait also attracts fish in murky or deep water. Anytime the fishing is difficult, use bait. Sunfish have an acute sense of smell, so the scent of the real thing is a powerful attractant.

Bait fishing is a study in simplicity. In most situations, you can thread the bait on a suitable hook, add just enough weight so it sinks, and then suspend it beneath a float. The trick is to get your bait to the same depth as the sunfish, which are usually within a couple of feet of the bottom. Active sunfish are ready biters, so if you don't have a bite within a few minutes, reel in and cast to a different spot.

Match your bait to the season. Early in the year, most food sources available to sunfish are small, so try grubs, angleworms, and mayfly nymphs. You can also break small pieces off a large nightcrawler. As summer progresses, add crickets, catalpa worms, grasshoppers, and very small leeches or minnows to the mix. Carefully hook the bait so it stays alive and adds enticing movement to your presentation. Where it is legal, you can chum an area with tiny bits of fish, bread, shrimp, or other foods to attract sunfish.

You can also catch sunfish on very small artificial lures, especially when the fish are very active. You can use tiny jigs, spinners, spinner-flies, spinnerbaits, and even pieces of pork rind or plastic worms. The advantage to artificial bait is that you don't have the fuss and mess of keeping and using natural bait. However, tipping a lure with a waxworm or small earthworm may increase your number of bites. Fish artificial bait as slowly as possible, because sunfish are unlikely to chase fast-moving bait.

Fly fishing for sunfish is top-notch fun. If the water is calm, try surface fishing with poppers or dry flies. Poppers festooned with life-like rubber legs are often the best producers. A foam-bodied popper may work better than a hard-bodied cork model, because the fish are less likely to reject it as a fake.

For subsurface action, try wet flies or nymphs. Colorful fly patterns that include yellow, red, or other bright colors often draw the most strikes.

Lures include: (1) popper, (2) Timberwolf, (3) Western Bee, (4) Emmy Jig with mealworm, (5) rubber spider, (6) Creme Angle Worm, (7) Beetle Spin, (8) Devil Spinner, (9) Panther Martin, (10) Black Fury Combo, (11) HalFly, (12) Road Runner, (13) Sassy Shad, (14) Jiggly.

Look for ripples, wakes, or other surface disturbances that reveal the location of spawners. Keep the sun at your back for best visibility of any panfish, including pumpkinseeds, whether spawning or not.

Fishing the Beds

Spawning sunfish concentrate in shallow areas and strike readily at baits that come close to their nests. Many anglers do the majority of their fishing for sunfish during the spawning period, because the action is fast and the fish are good sized. Male sunfish guard the nest and chase or attack anything that comes too close. Females continue to feed during the spawn.

Look for spawning areas along shorelines, where you may see the round nests on the bottom. Undeveloped shorelines are best. Areas where the lake bottom has been altered to create a swimming area or boat access usually lack adequate habitat.

Some anglers, particularly in the South, say they can smell spawning sunfish. Others believe the best fishing is within a few days of the full moon.

Sunfish may spawn in just a few inches of water or as deep as 15 feet (4.6 m), depending on water clarity and other conditions. Once you locate a spawning area, you'll probably find fish there year after year.

The timing of the spawn varies depending on latitude and the characteristics of an individual lake. In the South, sunfish begin spawning in February, while along the Canadian border it is possible to find fish on spawning beds as late as the Fourth of July. A shallow lake where the water temperature warms

quickly will have spawning activity days or weeks before a nearby deep, clear lake.

Once you locate sunfish nests, keep your distance as you fish. Otherwise, you may spook the spawners. Although they will soon return to their nests, they may be more wary and difficult to catch. Sometimes you can mark the location and return later.

When fishing, try not to cast so that your float lands with a plop on top of a nest. This will only spook the fish. Cast beyond the nests and slowly retrieve the bait over the fish. Strike quickly, because spawning sunfish are aggressive and may swallow the bait.

Pole slowly through a likely spawning
area or use an electric trolling motor. Look for
round, light-colored depressions on bottom.

Fishing Near Trees, Brush, and Vegetation

Since sunfish are prey for a host of predators, you'll often find them near cover. Flooded timber in reservoirs, fallen trees, brush piles, and beds of vegetation are good places to look for sunfish throughout the season. During the spawning season, you may find sunfish amidst brush in shoreline shallows. In summer, they may hold along the deep edge of the same or similar cover. Stumps, pilings, and bridge abutments will hold fish throughout the season.

When you fish near cover, expect your line to tangle once in awhile. Sometimes you can use a float to keep your bait above sunken branches or vegetation. You may be able to cast tiny jigs with light-wire hooks that are easy to pull free. Unfortunately, it is best to assume you will lose some hooks during the course of a day's fishing. Try not to let these problems frustrate you.

In many situations, anglers use a precise presentation to get their bait to the fish in heavy cover. You can use a long fishing rod or cane pole to lower your bait into pockets within the cover, beside tree stumps, or among brushy tangles. You may need to use a heavier line and extra weight to accomplish the task. When you hook a fish, play it quickly and firmly so it doesn't become tangled in the cover.

Dense aquatic vegetation presents special challenges, because it may be nearly impossible to find an opening to get your bait in the water. Use an oar or a length of aluminum conduit with a hook-shaped end to clear a hole in matted vegetation. Whenever possible, try to find fish along the edge of the cover, where it is easier to fish for them.

Many waters have productive, manmade cover, as well. Sometimes people sink pole- and-brush cribs, wooden stakes, or other objects in a lake or impoundment to attract fish. Often these locations are marked with buoys, or show up on depth maps. Anglers will likely find sunfish all around the attractor. Although you may hang up, try to keep your bait very close to the cover. Where law allows, you can even build and place your own fish attractors.

Docks, swimming platforms, bank stabilizers, and other objects also attract sunfish, especially those in deep water—more than 6 feet (1.8 m). Try fishing the shady portions of the dock or floating platform. Practice your casting so you can toss a bait beneath the dock. You can also use a long pole to precisely lower your bait near the cover. When fishing docks or similar cover, you may catch a few sunfish and then find that the action slows down. Move on and try another dock.

Drop your bait or lure straight down alongside a tree. If the tree has branches protruding at different depths cover them all thoroughly.

Cast beyond a large submerged tree (top), then let the line flow from the spool as the lure or bait sinks to bottom. Retrieve as close to the tree as possible.

Flick your lure or bait under a dock with an underhand motion (left). Or cast sidearm so your lure hits the water in front of the dock and skips under it.

Deep-water Sunfish

Sunfish may congregate along the deep edge of a point, hump, or similar submerged feature, especially in summer or during the bright light of day. Though most of the sunfish you find will be at depths of 10 to 15 feet (3.0 to 4.6 m), it pays to explore deeper water. Bluegills may be found deeper than 20 feet (6.1 m), while redear will descend to over 30 feet (9.1 m). Deep-water sunfish generally are larger fish. Because they are so deep and away from typical sunfish locations, few anglers target them.

If you find one structure sunfish, you should be able to find more of them. You will not likely find them tightly schooled; however, more sunfish should be holding at the same depth in the same or similar locations. Look for them adjacent to places where you find sunfish feeding early and late in the day. Usually, they will be within a foot or two of the bottom. Occasionally, sunfish suspend in open water.

Try casting or trolling along the edge of points or drop-offs to find deep-water sunfish. Fish very slowly and be sure to keep your bait near the bottom. When trolling, use an electric trolling motor for a quiet and controlled approach. Try very small spinners tipped with live bait, using just enough weight to keep your presentation near the bottom. Casters can motor slowly along the drop-off, casting 1/32 to 1/16 ounce (0.9 to 1.8 g) jigs to work the bottom.

Still-fishing with bait is a great way to thoroughly cover a good spot. Use an adjustable slip bobber to suspend your bait just above the bottom. What's great about using a slip bobber is that you know exactly how deep you are fishing and you have an efficient way to detect strikes. A small split shot should be sufficient to bring your bait to the proper depth.

You can also bait fish the bottom using a slip sinker held in place 12 to 24 inches (30.5 to 61.0 cm) from the hook with a tiny split shot. When you get a strike, the sunfish won't feel the resistance of the slip sinker. All baits may work in deep water situations, but proven favorites like small earthworms, crickets, small leeches, or grasshoppers are consistently effective.

Big bluegills and redear may be scattered in deep water and even suspended at mid depths. Catching such fish is very challenging. If you have a light to medium breeze, try drifting across likely spots using bait, small jigs, spinner-baits, or flies. Try near the bottom as well as at other depths until you begin catching fish.

You may be able to mark sunfish on your depth finder, which will help focus your search. Be forewarned—this midsummer strategy is a low odds game.

In some locales, anglers make a cheesecloth chum bag to attract sunfish. Use crushed snails or shrimp for chum. Put the chum into the bag along with enough rocks to sink it. Lower the bag on or near the bottom and fish in its near vicinity.

Points attract sunfish year-round. The fish usually hold near the tip of a point or around fingers projecting off the side.

Other Locations

Few fish are as widely distributed as sunfish. With careful fishing, enterprising anglers may discover overlooked sunfish. Look for waters where angler access is limited, such as the lack of road access or a boat ramp, private property, or proximity to nearby, better-known fishing holes. These lightly fished waters can produce out-sized sunfish.

People frequently stock sunfish in natural and manmade ponds. Some anglers seek permission to fish ponds located on private property, such as farms. You may also find ponds in public parks or recreation areas. Sometimes beavers will create a pond on a creek that contains sunfish, creating productive new habitat. The best ponds are ones in which people keep the sunfish population in balance within the small environs by stocking predators (such as largemouth bass) or by management (such as artificial feeding). Otherwise, the sunfish may overpopulate and become stunted.

If you own a float tube, canoe, or even a pair of hip boots, you can explore small waters that others pass by. Look for secluded bays or backwaters on large lakes and rivers. Smaller streams may contain sunfish in quiet pools, eddies, and slack water. Ditches and canals will hold sunfish, too. When the weather is cold, look for sunfish in slack water or places near warm-water discharges.

Savvy anglers learn to take advantage of occasional circumstances to catch big sunfish. A hatch of mayflies, flying ants, or other insects may trigger sunfish to feed ravenously. You may find sunfish congregated beneath overhanging trees and brush where caterpillars are dropping into the water. Summer breezes can blow grasshoppers and other flying insects into the lake.

Crush snails, grass shrimp, or saltwater shrimp, then put them inside a cheesecloth bag (above left). Add rocks for extra weight, then tie a long rope to the end of the bag.

Lower the bag until it is on or just above bottom, then fish close by (above right). If nothing happens in 10 minutes, move to another spot. Chum remains effective for about one hour. Add new chum when it no longer draws fish.

Chapter 4
Crappies

Crappies rank near the top with panfish anglers because they are easy to catch and live in a wide variety of waters. The two species are generally known as black crappies and white crappies, but anglers often refer to them by a variety of regional nicknames, such as specks, papermouths, bachelor perch, white perch, calico bass.

Black Crappie

Black crappies can be found throughout the United States and southern Canada, with the exception of the Rocky Mountains. Virtually everywhere the species is found, it is popular with anglers because it is abundant, easy to catch, and good to eat. You'll find crappies in natural lakes and reservoirs, as well as larger rivers and streams.

They continue feeding in cold water, which makes them a favorite quarry of ice anglers in northern states. They are also tolerant of brackish water and inhabit estuaries along the East and Gulf Coasts. Local names include papermouths, calico bass, specks, and sac a lait.

As its name suggests, the black crappie has erratic, mottled markings (which may be anywhere from black to green) over a body color ranging from silvery to a metallic green.

The coloration is especially pronounced during the spring spawning season, although crappies living in stained water generally have dark markings. The mottled coloration extends to the dorsal, anal, and caudal fins.

Another distinctive feature is their delicate mouths, which allows hooks to easily pull free if you apply too much pressure when playing one. Crappie mouths are shaped similarly to those of their near relatives, the black bass. As a result, they are able to eat larger prey, such as minnows.

Black crappies prefer waters with a hard sand or gravel bottom and some aquatic vegetation. They are mostly found in lakes, but also inhabit quiet areas in rivers and streams. Ranging farther north than their kin, the white crappie, black crappies are most abundant in cool, northern lakes.

Crappies spawn in the spring when the water temperature warms to about 65°F (18.3°C). In the Deep South, this may occur as early as January or it may be as late as June along the Canadian border. Generally, March and April are the spawning months throughout most of the black crappie range.

Schools of crappies build their nests in near-shore areas from 3 to 6 feet (0.9 to 1.8 m) deep, often adjacent to fallen trees or similar cover. Although they prefer to lay their eggs over a hard bottom substrate, crappies can spawn on mud, sand, shell beds, and submerged vegetation.

Spawning success varies from year to year. Biologists refer to the fish produced in an annual spawn as the year-class. The abundance of various year-classes within an overall crappie population determines both fishing success and the average size of fish caught by anglers. One abundant year-class can support a fishery for several years.

In northern lakes that black crappies share with walleyes, biologists have noted an interesting population dynamic. Generally, walleyes will dominate the lake fishery. However, if walleye numbers decline due to over fishing or some other factor, crappies will produce one or two excellent year-classes and proliferate. Black crappies will remain abundant until the walleye population recovers and then will decrease in numbers to their former population level.

Following the spawn, schools of crappies move to deeper water, often not far from their spawning areas. They may suspend off a point, sunken island, or the mouth of a bay. Throughout the year, the schools may move in search of forage, but you'll usually find them where the depth changes near cover or structure. On many waters, consistent "crappie holes" are well known to anglers. In the summer, you may see clusters of boats in the vicinity, while in the winter ice fishing "shanty towns" mark crappie hotspots.

The world record black crappie was caught in Louisiana's Westwago Canal in 1969, and weighed 6 pounds (2.72 kg). However, most crappies caught by anglers weigh 1 pound (0.5 kg) or less. Catch a black crappie topping 2 pounds (0.9 kg) and you most likely will get your picture with the fish published in the local paper. That said, dedicated crappie anglers seem to be on a never-ending quest for heavy "slabs." Because crappie populations reflect the abundance of various year-classes, the average size of fish in a particular lake may vary significantly from year to year.

■ Black Crappie Range

White Crappie

The white crappie is closely related to the black crappie, but generally has a more southern range. It is the only member of the sunfish family that has six spines in the dorsal fin and six spines in the anal fin, allowing for easy distinction from the black crappie, which has seven or eight dorsal spines. The white crappie is somewhat different in appearance, too. As the name suggests, it is lighter in coloration, with silvery-olive sides and a darker dorsal area. Most specimens have seven to nine dark, vertical bars along their flanks.

While both black and white crappies frequently occur in the same waters due to widespread stocking of both fish, they have somewhat different habitat preferences. White crappies can tolerate greater water turbidity and inhabit silty rivers and lakes. They are common in southern reservoirs.

Aside from a greater tolerance for murky water, white crappies have a similar life history to black crappies. Nest-builders, they spawn in the spring. Spawning success varies from year to year, leading to fluctuations in abundance. Crappies eat their own young, so a dominant year-class may suppress the following year-classes until its abundance dwindles.

White crappie numbers often explode following the creation of a new impoundment, because habitat is especially fertile. In such situations, they may also grow to exceptionally large sizes, reaching weights of 2 to 4 pounds (0.9 to 1.8 kg). An average-sized white crappie is less than 12 inches (30.5 cm) in length and weighs less than 1 pound (0.5 kg). The world record white crappie was caught at Mississippi's Enid Dam in 1957 and weighed 5 pounds, 3 ounces (2.35 kg).

White crappies are less likely to form tight schools than black crappies and are often located near cover. In the South, they prey heavily on gizzard and threadfin shad. In the northern part of their range, insects comprise a larger percentage of their diet. Although they suspend in the water column around mid-lake structure, you will also find white crappies on brushy shorelines and around submerged or flooded timber.

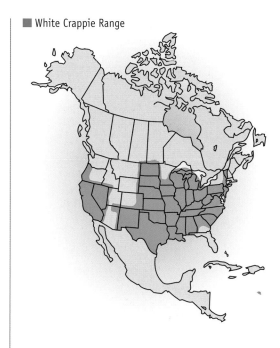

■ White Crappie Range

Where to Find Crappies

You'll find black and white crappies in similar locations. You might define their behavior as unpredictably predictable. Schools of crappies are often on the move, so you may find these rovers off a point or outside a bed of aquatic vegetation one evening and then draw a blank the next. Don't worry: If you've found a good spot, the crappies will soon be back. Crappie movements are seasonal, and they use different habitat throughout the year. The key to finding crappies is knowing where they should be in any given season.

In addition, you should also have an understanding of daily movements. Like many fish species, crappies move into shallower waters to feed during low light periods. They go deeper and are less active during the day. An exception is cold water. Then crappies are most active in the afternoon, when the sun has warmed the water. The arrival of a cold front may also put a chill in crappie activity. They usually go to deeper water and are difficult to catch until the front passes.

In natural lakes, crappie fishing kicks off in early spring, shortly after ice-out in northern states. Sunny days slowly warm the winter chill from the water, triggering pre-spawning activity. Look for crappies in shallow bays and flats with mud or dark bottoms, which absorb the warmth from sunlight. The north side of the lake has the best exposure to the sun and the water temperature may be several degrees warmer than the rest of the lake. The warming waters spur plankton growth, triggering a response throughout the food chain.

As the waters continue warming up, crappies begin moving toward spawning areas. Look for shallow areas less than 6 feet (1.8 m) deep that have gravel, sand, or rock bottoms. These may be sheltered shoreline areas or mid-lake humps and shoals. The best spawning sites usually have some aquatic vegetation. Brushy shorelines also attract spawners. In large lakes, spawning may begin earlier in sheltered locations where the water is warmest.

Following the spawn, crappies move to nearby edges, such as points, channel mouths, or just outside beds of aquatic

Boat harbors, channels and canals warm quickly in spring. Look for crappies along sunny shorelines protected from the wind.

Crappies often use brush piles for cover.

vegetation. Look for them along the breakline between shallow and deep water. As summer progresses, they move to deeper water, though they are still likely to relate to a break, drop-off, or vegetation edge. Sunken humps, rock piles, and other structure are good places to look for crappies, particularly if the edge is between 10 and 25 feet (3.0 and 7.6 m) deep. You may also find crappies suspended over open water of similar depths.

In the fall, crappies gradually return to shallower water. Look for schools along the outside edge of vegetation. Later, when the vegetation starts to die, you'll find them near rock piles and humps. As the water temperatures cool with the approach of winter, the crappies move to deep-water areas. They

will suspend at mid-depths and remain in these locations throughout the winter.

In impoundments, crappie movements are often associated with creek arms, coves, and inlets. Before the spring spawn, crappies begin moving into these areas from the main channel, because water flowing in from tributary creeks or in sheltered areas with sun exposure is warmer. As the spawn approaches, they will move farther into the creek arm, usually following the creek channel.

Spawning locations are often near flooded brush or timber in shallow water. By this time, the crappies have moved far into the arms, well away from the main channel. Look for spawners in the backs of coves, on shallow points or flats, and near small inlets. Spawning

sites are usually less than 5 feet (1.5 m) deep.

When the spawn is over, crappies slowly return to the main portion of the lake. Focus your search along the edge of the creek channel, looking for breaks and turns, as well as woody cover. When they reach the main channel, crappies will hold along the edge of drop-offs, particularly if there is flooded timber or similar cover nearby.

In the fall, crappies move back into the creek arms. Fishing can be excellent, because the fish are hungry. Look for them along the creek channel. When the water temperatures drop in late fall, the crappies return to the main lake. As in natural lakes, they'll seek deep-water wintering areas up to 40 feet (12.2 m) or more in depth.

Fishing Tactics

Crappies are extraordinarily popular with anglers because they are abundant and good to eat. Most of the fishing occurs at times of year when the fish are easy to catch, such as the spring spawning season or during the autumn bite. Anglers in northern states like to ice-fish for crappies, too.

When crappies are biting, they are not difficult to catch, but this doesn't mean they are pushovers. They are more wary than most panfish and will spook away from disturbances or noises. A little stealth goes a long way toward improving your crappie fishing success. Try to be quiet, keep your distance from the fish, and use the lightest gear possible. If the fish suddenly stop biting, they may have spooked or the school has simply moved. You may need to do the same if you want to keep catching fish.

Anglers catch the majority of crappies using small minnows for bait—a practical, four-season fishing method. Crappies also strike artificial lures and can provide challenging, fast action for anglers who enjoy casting. Fly fishing for crappies is a specialized activity that can be productive when crappies are in shallow water, such as during the spawn, or feeding near the surface.

Far more common, especially in the South, is the tight-line method, where anglers use a heavy sinker beneath a tandem or multiple hook bait rig so they can lower it vertically into woody or rocky cover. You can also use extra-long crappie poles or cane poles to fish in heavy cover.

When fishing for crappies, take it slow and easy. Crappies are more likely to take slow-moving bait rather than a quick retrieve. Strikes are often barely perceptible, so watch your float or fishing line for the slightest indication of movement.

Crappies have very soft mouths, so just raise the rod tip to set the hook. Play the fish carefully and keep a tight line or the hook will fall out or tear free. Bring a landing net for the same reason. When you play a crappie to boat side or the bank, be ready with a waiting net. Bring the fish over the net, and then lift the net.

Crappies strike a variety of baits, though minnows less than 2 inches (5 cm) long are the most popular. Bait shops usually sell these small minnows as "crappie minnows," which are readily available. Lively minnows work best, so make sure your minnow container has cool, fresh, well-oxygenated water. You can buy stress-

Cane poles or telescopic fiberglass poles should be stiff enough to hoist fish out of openings in cover. Most anglers use 12- to 16-foot (3.7 to 4.9 m) poles, then tie on a length of monofilament several feet longer than the pole. Some extension poles have built-in reels. The angler threads the line through the inside of the pole and out the tip.

reducing chemicals to add to the water in order to keep your minnows alive. If you are fishing for large crappies, you may find slightly larger minnows are more effective. If two sizes or species of minnows are available at the bait shop, buy some of both because one may out-produce the other.

When fishing with a minnow, carefully hook it so that it remains alive. Use small or light-wire hooks. Hook the minnow just ahead of the tail or beneath the dorsal fin when using floats or still fishing. When casting or trolling, hook the minnow through the lips so that it moves naturally through the water. If you are not getting bites, try changing your minnow. Sometimes a freshly baited minnow draws strikes.

Crappies also bite on worms, leeches, small cut baits, grasshoppers, insects, grass shrimp, and other baits. You can buy a variety of commercial products, including preserved natural baits, artificial grubs, and scented doughs for crappie fishing.

Some veteran crappie anglers swear by jigs. Casting small jigs dressed with marabou, bucktail, plastic tube tails, or twister tails is an excellent way to thoroughly cover an area. You can attach a tiny spinnerbait blade for greater attraction. You'll also find that you can tip the jig with a lip-hooked minnow, too. You don't need to fish the jig on the bottom. Make a twitching retrieve with the jig at the depths where the crappies are holding. Tiny crankbaits, spinners, and jigging spoons also catch crappies.

Flooded brush provides spawning cover in many reservoirs. Crappies also spawn in seasonally flooded brush in river backwaters.

Fishing for Spawning Crappies

Crappies are ready biters during the spawn, but you must approach the shallow spawning sites quietly and present your bait within the few inches of the bedding fish. You can do this by casting and retrieving a jig, by precisely placing your bait with an extended crappie pole, or by fishing with a minnow suspended beneath a float. When you get a strike, pay attention to the depth you were fishing. Crappies will seldom take a bait off the bottom or rise more than a few inches to strike.

If the water is clear, you may be able to see the crappies. If you quietly move your boat through spawning areas, you may spook the fish off their beds. You can return and fish for them a short time later. More likely, you'll need to carefully work a likely area to find unseen spawners.

In brush, vegetation, or timber, dangle your bait close to the cover. Use ultra-light tackle whenever possible. In heavy cover, you may need to use a heavy line and a medium-weight rod so you can hoist the fish before it tangles your line in the cover.

In open areas, you can catch fish by fly-casting small streamers and wet flies. Use a weighted fly or slow-sinking fly line to make presentations at the right depth.

Stumps and logs attract spawning crappies. Look for the largest stumps and those with root systems that have been washed free of soil.

Look for brush patches, standing timber, fallen trees, stumps or any other type of woody cover along a shoreline (above). Fish one piece of cover for a few minutes, then move on to the next. You will usually catch more crappies by covering a large area than by staying in one spot.

Drop your bait into openings between the roots of a tree (right). A crappie will often hold tight in a small crevice and refuse to bite unless you dangle the bait directly in front of its nose.

Fishing in Cover

If you can find some wood in the water, often you'll find crappies. Fallen trees, flooded brush, stump fields, roots, and standing timber are excellent crappie habitat. Baitfish, aquatic insects, and other food sources are readily available. Brush and trees provide shade and shelter from predators.

Crappies congregate near shallow brush and trees during the spawn, but remain close to flooded trees and stumps in deeper water throughout the summer. The trick to catching them is to get your bait very close to the cover. Use light-wire hooks that will straighten and pull free if you hang up. You can also use heavier line, because it is less noticeable to the fish amid branches and vegetation.

Anglers in the South use tight-line rigs with tandem hooks to work heavy cover. You can also suspend a bait or a small jig beneath a float. Twitch the float to impart motion to your offering. Keep your casts short so that you have control of your line, which helps you avoid frequent hang-ups.

In natural lakes, you'll often find crappies near beds of vegetation. Crappies move into vegetation during the bright light of day and feed along the edges during low-light periods. Vegetation with wide leaves, commonly called cabbage, provides better cover than dense, narrow-leaved aquatic plants. In the fall, seek out areas where the plants are still green, rather than those where the plants have begun to die and decay. With some experience, you will learn to recognize the plants and locations most likely to hold crappies.

Fishing near vegetation requires patience and practice for you to become proficient at placing your bait without hanging up. Look for pockets in the cover or irregular edges where the crappies can hide and come out to take your bait. If the vegetation is beneath the water's surface, you can swim an artificial lure just above it or suspend a minnow beneath a float. Some anglers cast small spinnerbaits and then pause their retrieve so the lure slowly sinks. Crappies often strike as the bait falls.

Fishing Structure

Rock piles, sunken islands, long tapering points, and the break line of an irregular shoreline are good places to look for crappies on natural lakes. In reservoirs, you can also find them along submerged channels. Locate structure using an electronic depth finder.

During the day, crappies are likely to hold along the edge of the drop offs or suspend in adjacent deep water. In the evening, they may move up on the structure to feed.

When you fish structure, keep moving until you locate active fish. Often the best way to do this is by trolling along the break line with a spinner and minnow combination, a jig and minnow, or a small crankbait. As you troll, pay close attention to your depth finder, because the crappies often hold at a specific depth or in specific locations.

When you catch one, you may be able to anchor and then cast or still-fish to find others. Tossing out an anchor may spook the fish, so consider using an electric trolling motor to hold your position. If the crappies are scattered, continuing to troll may be more effective.

In many lakes and reservoirs, people place manmade structures to attract crappies and other fish species. These structures include sunken brush or Christmas trees, beds of upright stakes, and large wooden cribs. If a fish management agency built the structure, the location is usually marked on lake maps or identified with floating markers. Sometimes local anglers sink attractors themselves. Unless someone tells you where the attractors are located, you may not find them.

Approach structures quietly (using an electric trolling motor is best) and fish your bait close to or in the cover. The structures are usually not very large, so the crappies will be concentrated. You may catch only one or two fish from a small structure. If people have placed a

Bridge pilings provide shade for crappies, especially if they have numerous cross-members. Algae growth on wooden pilings draws insects that attract baitfish.

number of structures in the vicinity, move on and try another when the fish stop biting.

Structures located in water less than 10 feet (3.0 m) deep will be most productive in early morning and the evening, while those in deeper water may hold crappies throughout the day.

Docks, riprap, boat harbors, bridges, and boathouses offer food and cover to crappies. Casting jigs or still fishing with a minnow tight to the cover is productive. Some locations, such as riprap and manmade harbors, warm up more quickly in the spring, attracting pre-spawn crappies. Bridge abutments and pilings in deeper water may hold crappies throughout the summer.

In some places, people secure floating structures over good fishing spots. Operators charge a fee for anglers to sit inside these fishing lounges and fish in relative comfort. These are great places to take children or elderly folks fishing.

Rock piles that top off at 12 to 20 feet (3.7 to 6.1 m) hold crappies in summer. Algae on the rocks harbor tiny insect larvae that attract baitfhish, which then draw crappies.

Standing timber offers good crappie habitat. Crappies find cover in treetops, among limbs and branches along the trunk and in exposed roots. Trees with bare trunks seldom hold crappies.

Suspended Crappies

During the summer, it may be difficult to find crappies near cover, especially during the day. Often the fish are suspended at moderate depths, away from structure or cover. The only way to find them is to start searching and cover some water. If you have a moderate wind, try drifting across likely areas with a minnow on a hook and sinker rig. You can control the depth at which you are fishing by the length of line and the weight of your sinker.

If you hook a crappie, immediately toss out a marker buoy so you can find the spot again. Suspended crappies may be holding at the same depth or scattered at various depths. Often you can see them on your depth finder and determine the depths.

You can also find suspended or scattered crappies by trolling with a spinner and minnow, a jig and minnow, a nightcrawler harness, or similar rig. Again, control the depth at which you are fishing by the length of line and amount of weight you are using. Once you locate suspended crappies, try to fish for them by casting a jig or fishing with a float and minnow. Use a slip bobber when fishing depths of 5 feet (1.5 m) or more to make casting easier.

Crappies After Dark

Night fishing for crappies is a popular summertime pursuit, especially during hot weather. The fish feed actively at night, and the air temperature is cool and comfortable. Where law allows, anglers use lanterns to attract crappies, which swim to the minnows feeding on tiny organisms beneath the lights. A dark night is best for fishing with lights. You can use a camping lantern for light or buy a floating lantern designed for night fishing. The latter is less likely to attract insect pests.

Set up in a location near cover or structure that holds crappies. Often anglers fish from docks, fishing piers, or other spots that offer easy access from shore. Fish with a float and minnow and try fishing anywhere from a couple feet beneath the surface to near the bottom. Lighted bobbers are easier to see in the dark and add a little excitement to the fishing. When the light begins to move and then disappears, you have a bite.

Suspended crappies can be difficult to locate because they follow and feed on schools of roaming minnows.

Chapter 5
Yellow Perch

A nglers have a love-hate relationship with the yellow perch. In the North, when walleyes are biting, anglers consider small yellow perch that take the bait a nuisance. However, other anglers elevate yellow perch to a cult-like status, pursuing them throughout the year as the main ingredient for fish fries. Anglers who are fishing for other species can sometimes avoid small perch by changing locations or using larger bait.

60

YELLOW PERCH

Few will dispute that yellow perch are among the best tasting freshwater fish. This isn't surprising, because they are members of the Percidae family that includes walleye and sauger. What they may lack in size when compared with walleyes, yellow perch make up for with abundance. Fast action is the name of the game when you fish for yellow perch.

The yellow perch is widely distributed throughout the northern and eastern United States and much of Canada. Although stocking has expanded their range, they are not found in the warm waters of the South. Primarily a lake-dwelling fish, it prefers cool, clear water with a sandy or rocky bottom. Yellow perch are an important species throughout the Great Lakes, though they are confined to shallow bays and estuaries in cold, deep Lake Superior. They also inhabit brackish waters along the Atlantic Coast. They range northward to Hudson's Bay.

The yellow perch is a handsome fish. The coloration may range from vivid to pale depending on the time of year and the water body. Olive-green vertical bars enhance a yellow, elongated body. Bright-yellow to orange pectoral and anal fins add a pleasing accent of color. The perch has two dorsal fins. Handle them carefully, because the front dorsal fin contains sharp spines.

In most waters, yellow perch are an important prey species for larger predators, especially walleyes. In part, this is because the average perch is just a few inches in length. Young perch comprise a sizeable portion of the population. Growing at a rate of 2 or 3 inches (5 to 7.6 cm) annually, a yellow perch must survive three or four years of predation before it grows large enough for anglers. Generally 8- to 10-inch (20.3 to 25.4 cm) perch are considered "keepers" and weigh from 1/4 to 1/2 pound (0.1 to 0.2 kg). Larger perch, called "jumbos" may be 12 to 14 inches (30.5 to 35.6 cm) long and weigh 1 pound (0.5 kg) or more. Not all waters produce jumbo perch and those that do attract anglers from far and wide. In some lakes, yellow

perch are so prolific that they become stunted and are of little value. The world record dates to 1865, weighs 4 pounds, 3 ounces (1.89 kg), and was caught in New Jersey's Delaware River. However, all of the other record yellow perch listed by the Freshwater Fishing Hall of Fame weigh less than 3 pounds (1.4 kg).

Perch spawn at night in the spring when water temperatures reach 43 to 50°F (6.1 to 10.0°C). The female lays a gelatinous strand of eggs about 1 inch (2.5 cm) wide and several inches long that becomes draped or imbedded in bottom vegetation or debris. In about two weeks the eggs hatch and release thousands of tiny fry. As they grow, the young perch form huge schools that provide forage for predators. Although you will frequently see small perch in shoreline shallows, especially near cover, they also move out to deeper water.

Feeding first on tiny aquatic organisms, perch gradually switch to a diet of minnows, leeches, insects, and crustaceans as they grow. Throughout its life, the perch remains a schooling fish and schools are usually comprised of similar-sized fish. In most basins, they roam the lake in search of food, typically staying close to the bottom.

■ Yellow Perch Range

Where to Find Yellow Perch

Keeper-size yellow perch are not abundant in all waters. Start your search for perch in a lake known to produce jumbos. Otherwise, your fishing effort may be a lesson in futility. Remember, too, that perch of similar size usually school together. If you are catching only small ones, move to another location. Perch have a couple of unusual characteristics. They often feed most heavily at midday and cold fronts have less influence on yellow perch activity than they do on most other panfish.

In early spring, perch leave their deep wintering areas and head for the places where they will spawn. On big water, this spring migration may cover a distance of several miles or more. Spawning areas have a hard bottom of sand, gravel, or rock, usually at depths of 5 to 12 feet (1.5 to 3.7 m). In large bodies of water, they may spawn at greater depths. The spawning site may have sparse vegetation or brush on the bottom.

Yellow perch living in brackish estuaries along the Atlantic coast spawn in tributary streams, often running upstream until they are blocked by a dam. Stream spawning may

occur in shallow areas 2 to 3 feet (0.6 to 0.9 m) deep.

Following the spawn, yellow perch may linger in the vicinity for several weeks, until the water temperatures become too warm. Then they begin moving deeper to find their preferred water temperature, which is less than 70°F (21.1°C).

During the summer, you will find them along the thermocline, the area which has the coolest water containing suffi-cient oxygen. Although they may suspend just above the thermocline, you are more likely to find them at the depth where the thermocline meets the bottom. In the Great Lakes, where cooler water is more available, yellow perch retreat to depths of 20 to 30 feet (6.1 to 9.1 m), moving into shallower water in the evening to feed. In brackish estuaries, yellow perch school in the deep holes of spawning tributaries during the summer.

As water temperatures cool during the fall, yellow perch start moving toward shallower water. Look for them in areas with a rocky or hard bottom.

Great Lakes anglers catch them by fishing from piers. Estuary perch may move upstream in tributaries or linger in deep water. Fishing action slows as winter arrives to locales that remain ice-free. However, ice-fishing for perch is excellent in northern lakes.

Piers and breakwalls extending into water 20 feet (6.1 m) or deeper attract Great Lakes perch in spring and fall. The fish move out of deep water to spawn among rocks on the inshore end of a pier.

Fishing Tactics

If you catch one jumbo perch, you'll likely land enough of them for a meal or two. They travel in schools and a struggling fish on the end of your line will often attract others. For this reason, perch anglers use multiple-hook rigs where legal. If you are using a single hook, quickly get your line back in the water when the bite is on. Very likely, you'll immediately catch another fish.

As any angler who has been annoyed with tiny, bait-stealing perch knows, they are voracious eaters. Small perch often go after surprisingly large baits. However, yellow perch have comparatively small mouths, so they may, in essence, bite off more than they can chew. For this reason, #6 or #4 hooks and small- to moderate-size baits are usually the most effective.

Sometimes, perch will nibble at a bait or start swimming away with it, yet not take the hook in their mouth. If you are missing bites and reeling in chewed-up baits, try pulling the bait away from the fish when you feel a bite. It may strike more aggressively to prevent the bait from escaping.

You can catch yellow perch on small artificial lures, but bait is usually best. Minnows, worms and leeches are productive, but you can use various insects, cut bait, or crutaceans, too. Often a piece of a nightcrawler or a minnow catches more yellow perch than a whole one. However, if the perch are finicky, a lively minnow or worm will draw strikes.

Perch are attracted to bright colors. Try threading a bright-colored bead on your fishing line just above the hook. For extra flash, add a spinner.

Spring and Fall Fishing

Spring is a favorite time for many yellow perch anglers, because the spawning fish are congregated in shallow water and bite readily. You can find them by seeking out likely areas with a hard bottom or, perhaps more easily, looking for gatherings of perch anglers. On the Great Lakes and other large inland waters, you'll see anglers fishing from piers and break-walls. Out East, look for anglers on estuary tributaries. When the water cools in the fall, the same places and techniques become productive.

Most of the food sources eaten by spawning perch are small, because spring is the start of the growing season. You'll find small baits work best. Try a crappie minnow fished beneath a float. Where they are allowed, multiple-hook rigs are popular. The weight is tied to the end of the line and short dropper lines with hooks are tied-in above at intervals of 6 inches (15.25) or so.

Commercial spreader rigs use light, stiff wire to spread the baits away from the main line. On the East Coast, jigs called shad darts are baited with grass shrimp or minnows and fished beneath a float. Sometimes, anglers tie a small spoon to the end of the line and fish the dart on a dropper. If the yellow perch are finicky, try an ice fly tipped with larva.

Add several strands of bright red yarn to the shank of a plain hook or small jig. Wrap the yarn with winding thread to hold it in place. The bright color has special appeal to perch, especially during a feeding frenzy.

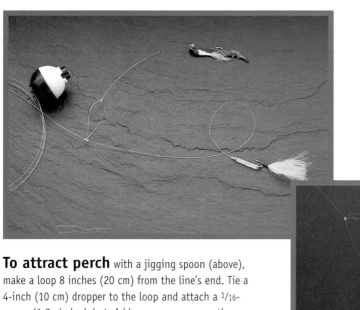

To attract perch with a jigging spoon (above), make a loop 8 inches (20 cm) from the line's end. Tie a 4-inch (10 cm) dropper to the loop and attach a 1/16-ounce (1.7 g) shad dart. Add a no-name spoon, then clip on a small float. Bait the dart with a grass shirmp.

Adjust the float so the spoon rides about 2 inches off bottom (right). Cast, let the rig settle, then reel back slowly with occasional twitches followed by pauses. The fluttering spoon will draw fish to the dart.

Weeds and submerged branches along protected shorelines provide ideal spawning habitat, especially in natural lakes. Perch mill around these areas before spawning, then drape their eggs over the vegetation.

To attract perch with a jigging spoon (above), remove the hook from a jigging lure, then tie the lure to your line. Add 12 inches (30 cm) of 6-pound (2.7 kg) mono to the split-ring at the bottom of the lure. Attach a #4 or #6 hook and a minnow hooked through the lips.

Lower the jigging spoon until it touches bottom, then reel up several inches (right). Jig the lure up and down to attract yellow perch to the minnow. Set the hook immediately when you feel a bite.

Summer Fishing

In some regions, yellow perch fishing slacks off during the summer. This isn't due to difficult fishing, but because the perch may have unattractive parasites in their flesh. The incidence of parasites may vary from one lake to the next. If you like to fish for perch, you can probably find waters where the fish have few parasites. And in many places, summer parasites are of little concern to yellow perch fanatics.

Summer perch fishing occurs away from shore, where schools of jumbos roam in water that may be from 20 to over 30 feet (6.1 to over 9.1 m) deep. You may find them feeding around hard-bottom humps and reefs, though they also move out on mud flats to feed on the nymphs of mayflies and other aquatic insects. Occasionally, you may find them suspended and actively feeding.

Slow-troll or drift with bait near the bottom to locate yellow perch. Add a bright-colored spinner for extra attraction. When you start catching fish, toss out a marker buoy. You can continue trolling in the vicinity or anchor and cast. Try fishing a jig or jigging spoon tipped with bait just off the bottom. Still-fishing with bait, either over the side of the boat or beneath a slip bobber is effective, too.

Yellow perch have a sense of curiosity. Enterprising anglers use various methods to attract them. You can bang or scrape the bottom with chunks of metal or a cement block lowered on a rope to create commotion. You can also tie colored plastic flags to your anchor rope. Chumming with cut bait may bring them in. Regardless of the tricks you try, if they don't work or the fish stop biting, keeping moving until you find action.

Yellow perch are drawn to bright colors. Lake Erie anglers often attach flags to their anchor ropes to attract them.

Chapter 6
White Bass

White bass belong to the temperate bass family, which includes striped bass, yellow bass, and white perch. Vorocious feeders that travel in large schools, white bass generate excitement when the bite is on.

Occasionally, a school of hungry white bass will chase baitfish to the surface in their predatory attack. The splashing commotion attracts gulls, which also feed on the hapless minnows. Anglers follow the dive-bombing gulls to take part in the explosive surface fishing action. The average white bass weighs 1 to 2 pounds (0.5 to 0.9 kg), but the world record, caught in Michigan's Saginaw Bay in 1989, weighed 6 pounds, 7 ounces (2.91 kg).

Fish culturists have created a white bass/striped bass hybrid that grows larger and has been stocked in many waters. The striper hybrid, or "wiper," isn't really a panfish, because it commonly attains weights from 10 to 20 pounds (4.5 to 9.1 kg). A near relative, the yellow bass, is similar in size and characteristics to the white bass, but has a much smaller

■ Striped Bass Range
■ White Bass Range
■ Combined Range

range. The yellow bass is native to the central United States.

When you think of white bass, think big water. Originally native to the Great Lakes and Mississippi River system, white bass have been stocked in reservoirs and big lakes throughout the South and Southwest. Although they thrive in some large rivers, white bass do best in large, clear-water lakes. Unlike members of the sunfish family, they are most at home in the open lake. Gizzard and threadfin shad are their favorite prey, though they will feed upon other baitfish, as well as crustaceans, mollusks, and insects.

White bass spawn in the spring when the water temperature reaches 60°F (15.6°C).

They prefer to spawn over gravel or rubble on shoals, shorelines, or tributary streams in places where current or wave action washes over the eggs. Females do not build nests, but broadcast from 25,000 to one million eggs on the bottom. Peak spawning activity usually occurs over a five- to ten-day period, then the adults return to their big-water habitat. Not every spawn is successful; a strong year-class occurs about once every three or four years. The newly hatched fry form massive schools that immediately begin feeding.

In productive habitat, white bass may measure 5 to 8 inches (12.7 to 20.3 cm) in length by the end of their first summer.

The fast growth continues until they reach maturity at age three or four. A 13-inch (33.0-cm) white bass may weigh about 1 pound (0.5 kg) and a 16-incher (40.6-cm) about 2 pounds (0.9 kg). They typically live six years.

Schooling behavior is a life-long characteristic. White bass roam the lake in a constant search for food. During the day, they may retreat to deeper water, cruising into the shallows during low-light periods. Unpredictability may be their only predictable characteristic when it comes to locating white bass. Fisheries' researchers have found that tagged white bass may move up to 100 miles (161 km) from their original tagging site.

Where to Find White Bass

In the spring, white bass become active when the water temperature reaches 50°F (10°C). Schools gather near the mouths of tributary streams in preparation for spawning. Soon they begin migrating upstream. Males take the lead, often reaching the spawning area up to a week ahead of the females. The run may slow or even recede downstream in response to rainstorms or cold fronts that roil or chill the water. Like most stream-spawning species, white bass go as far upstream as possible, stopping only when a dam, waterfall, or impassable shallows block their way. Spawning activity peaks when the water temperature tops 55°F (12.8°C). Huge schools swarm below the barrier, spawning on rocks, riprap, and sand bottoms in water up to 10 feet deep (3.0 m).

When the spawn is over, males and females begin drifting downstream. As they recover from the spawn, they'll hold in the lower portions or off the mouths of tributaries for a period of time before returning to the lake or reservoir. Once they reach the main body of the lake, white bass remain in roving schools. Finding them during the summer can be challenging,

Stripers and white bass thrive in Kentucky's Lake Cumberland and other southern reservoirs.

When white bass are schooled up, you can easily catch several of them in a short time. This fast-paced surface action took place on Elephant Butte Lake, New Mexico.

although they may follow channels, submerged roads, or other underwater pathways. When the thermocline forms, they suspend in the cool water along its upper edges.

White bass prey upon baitfish, especially large schools of shad. Throughout the warm months, you may see them breaking the surface early and late in the day as they chase shad. They may push the fleeing baitfish onto a shallow flat or against flooded brush and timber to corral them. Anglers look for them along the drop-off of a mud or sand bar formed at the mouth of a tributary. White bass also feed at night and anglers catch them in hard-bottom areas ranging from 10 to 20 feet (3 to 6.1 m) deep. Bridges or points that constrict the width of a lake or reservoir are good places to look for them.

As winter nears, white bass move toward deeper water, though they continue aggressively feeding on shad and other baitfish in the shallows and near the surface. As water temperatures cool, they become less active and spend more time in deep water. They are difficult to catch once the water temperature falls below 50°F (10°C). In winter, the best white bass fishing is in the warm outflow of power plant discharges.

WHITE BASS

Fishing Tactics

White bass fishing is exciting. When the bite is on, look out! Schools of white bass are frenetic feeders as they attack their prey. Nevertheless, the frenzy can soon be over if you spook the school. Be quiet and keep your distance when working active fish. The best times to fish for white bass are during stable weather periods or on overcast days.

Light tackle anglers consider white bass to be very sporting fish. They are surprisingly strong and may even break your line during the battle. This is because they have sharp gill covers that can easily slice through monofilament. Check your line frequently for nicks and abrasions. Also, be careful to avoid those sharp gill plates when handling the fish. Either lift them by the lower lip or grasp firmly around the body.

Light spinning tackle matched with 6- to 8-pound-test (2.7- to 3.6-kg) line is a good choice. Set your drag so a fish can take line if it makes a run. If your drag is set too tight, the fish can get leverage against the rod and twist or tear free.

You don't need a net to land white bass, but learn how to lift the fish from the water and swing it into the boat or on shore with one fluid motion so it doesn't have a chance to shake free.

Size matters when selecting white bass lures. Very often, the fish only strike lures that are the same size as their prey. Sometimes finding the right lure involves some guesswork, but attentive anglers can look for clues. If you are after surface-feeding white bass, you

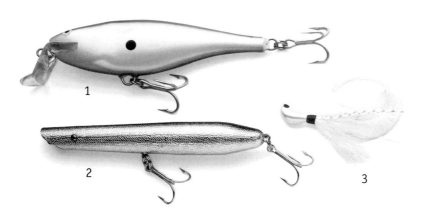

Lures for jump-fishing
(see page 78) include: (1) plugs, such as the Normark Super Shad Rap; (2) popping plugs, such as the Cordell Pencil Popper; (3) jigs, such as the Northland Bucktail Jig, tipped with a curlytail grub; (4) topwaters, such as the Heddon Tiny Torpedo; (5) tailspins, such as Mann's Little George; and (6) jigs, such as the Mister Twister Sassy Shad.

White bass fishermen attach a ¼-inch by 1¼-inch-long (0.6 by 3.2 cm) strip of belly meat to the jig when fishing is slow.

may see dead or injured shad floating near the surface, or the fish you catch may regurgitate their prey.

A white bass angler's tackle box may contain just about anything, but it is sure to have an assortment of jigs and other weighted lures, such as tail-spins. Jigs and tailspins offer versatility. You can fish them shallow or deep, they have plenty of action, they are easy to cast, and they come in an assortment of colors and sizes.

Using a jig, you can cast to white bass feeding on the surface or search for them in deeper water. Tailspins and jigs that incorporate a spinner blade get the nod from many anglers. The spinner adds fish-attracting flash and slows the descent of a sinking lure.

In deep-water situations, jigging spoons, vibrating blades, and similar lures for vertical presentations are effective.

Use crankbaits for quickly covering the water when prospecting for schools or working scattered fish. Carry a selection ranging from shallow-runners to deep-divers. Sound attracts white bass, so rattling crankbaits are a good choice.

Surface plugs are fun to use, because white bass frequently make explosive strikes. You can use them when fish are visibly feeding on the surface or to draw them to the top.

In some situations, you can catch white bass on flies. Try streamer patterns that imitate shad fished on a sinking line. During a hatch of mayflies or other insects, try nymphs or dry flies with a floating line. You can also tie a fly or small jig to a short length of line (about 12 inches/30.5 cm) and fish it as a trailer behind another lure.

Spring Fishing for White Bass

Spring is the best time to catch large numbers of white bass, because they are concentrated in spawning areas. If you know where the fish are likely to be before, during, and after the spawn, you can have several weeks of excellent fishing. In most waters, spawning white bass run up rivers or streams, although they will spawn on lake gravel bars that are 5 to 10 feet (1.5 to 3.0 m) deep. Prior to spawning, they stage near the tributary or begin swimming upstream. Fish for them along the edge of the current in eddies, bays, behind points and wing dams, and downstream of fallen trees or other current obstructions, generally in water less than 15 feet (4.6 m) deep. They may go deeper in response to a cold front.

Use water temperature as a guide to locating prespawn fish. White bass become active when the water rises above 50°F (10°C). Spawning begins when the temperature reaches the high 50s (up to 15.6°C). By then, the fish will be in spawning areas below dams or in shallow eddies just off the main current. Not all of the fish spawn at once, so you can fish for spawners during a period that may last several days or a couple of weeks. Often, you can see or hear white bass splashing on the surface as they go through the spawning ritual. Most spawning occurs during twilight or after dark. You can catch fish at night by casting toward the splashing sounds.

In most spawning locations you can either fish from a boat or from shore. In fact, spring is the best time of year for bank fishing. Small lures usually work best. Jigs are a good choice, because they sink at a consistent rate and you can control them in the current. They are also inexpensive to replace if you hang up on the bottom and break your line. Spawning white bass often attract many anglers. If you are new to white bass fishing, pay attention to where successful anglers are fishing and the methods they use.

Topwater lures for white bass include: (1) stickbaits, such as the Heddon Zara Puppy; (2) propbaits, such as the Cotton Cordell Crazy Shad; (3) floating minnow plugs, such as the Cotton Cordell Redfin; and (4) popping plugs, such as the Cotton Cordell Pencil Popper.

Trolling Tips

Choose gizzard shad (bottom) instead of threadfin shad (top) whenever possible. Gizzard shad work better for bait because they are hardier and grow to a larger size. You can distinguish between the two by differences in coloration. The gizzard shad has a blackish margin on the tail; the threadfin, yellowish. To keep shad lively while trolling, push the hook through the shad's nostrils. Use a 2- to 3-ounce (56 to 85 g) egg sinker about 4 feet (1.2 m) above the hook to get the shad down deep.

Make a spreader rig by bending a piece of stiff wire as shown. A spreader enables you to troll three jigs at a time on a single line and keeps them tracking far enough apart so they don't tangle.

Trolling lures for white bass include: (1) crankbaits, such as the Storm ThinFin; (2) vibrating plugs, such as the Cordell Super Spot; (3) horsehead jigs, such as the Hyper Striper Stump Jumper; and (4) minnow baits, such as the Cotton Cordell Red Fin.

Summer Fishing for White Bass

After the spawn, white bass return to the main lake or reservoir. Schools comprised of similar-size fish will be on the move, seeking shad. Summertime fishing isn't as consistent as fishing during the spawn, but it can be very exciting when you connect with a hungry school. If the fish are in deep water, this may not be easy. White bass don't necessarily relate to structure, so you may need to cover some water to find them. Try trolling along submerged channels or near the edges of points or humps. Watch your depth finder for marks depicting fish or baitfish.

During hot weather, fish at night. Place a lantern or light near the water to attract baitfish. White bass and likely crappies will follow, though perhaps not immediately. If you have a good spot—preferably one where you or someone else has caught them before—be

patient. Eventually, a school will show up. Pay attention to the time. You can probably return around the same time the next night for another white bass rendezvous. Use minnows fished beneath a light bobber for consistent success, though white bass also strike artificial lures.

Jump-fishing is the most exciting way to catch white bass in summer and fall. Voracious schools of white bass chase baitfish, often shad, to the surface and then slashingly attack them. The commotion and the easy pickings of injured prey attract flocks of gulls. Anglers spot the gulls and motor over for fast fishing action. Jump-fishing is best when the surface is relatively calm—usually early and late in the day.

Jump-fishing offers fast action, but don't take it for granted. Surface-feeding white bass are skittish and the school will sound if you disturb it. Approach the school from

upwind. Shut the motor off some distance away from the feeding activity and coast to within reasonable casting distance. Have your rod rigged and ready to cast. You may want to have a second rod rigged with a different lure in case you break your line or want to try a different presentation.

Cast into the commotion and keep your lure near the surface. When you hook a fish, its struggles will attract other white bass. If your partner places a cast nearby, he or she may hook one as well. When the school sounds, switch to deep-running lures or a vertical jigging presentation. Hungry white bass are likely lurking beneath the surface. When you see a flock of gulls on the water, try fishing beneath them. Sometimes you can draw fish back to the surface by noisily chugging a topwater lure where they were feeding. Make the most of the fast action by tying a trailer jig to your lure.

Watch for gulls swooping down to catch injured shad, or look for white bass breaking the surface. Many anglers use binoculars to spot the action from a distance.

Winter Fishing for White Bass

When water temperatures cool in late fall, white bass move to deep-water wintering areas. They are much less active and no longer roam the lake in search of food. Catching them isn't easy. Locate schools with your depth finder and try to tempt them with vertical pre-sentations.

In reservoirs that contain striped bass or white bass-striped bass hybrids, winter anglers troll the depths using downriggers or lead-core line.

You can also try winter fishing in the outflow of warm-water discharges. The water temperature is consistent and may top 50°F (10°C). White bass go to discharge areas to feed on shad and other baitfish that prefer warmer water temperatures. Cast with jigs or crankbaits. Fishing a minnow beneath a bobber may reward you with a mixed bag of fish.

In southern states, you can catch white bass beneath dam tailraces throughout much of the winter.

Chapter 7
Regional Panfish Species

Some panfish species have specific habitat needs that limit their geographic distribution. Cold-water species, such as whitefish and cisco, are limited to the northern tier of states and Canada. Others, such as the Rio Grande perch, cannot tolerate cool temperatures and exist only in the southernmost waters in the Lower 48. Where they are found, regional panfish species may be angling novelties or common local favorites.

Rock Bass

Your regard for rock bass may largely depend on where you first encountered them. In the North, anglers in pursuit of smallmouth bass or walleyes consider the rock bass a nuisance at best. Popular in the mountain streams of the Ozarks, anglers call rock bass goggleye or redeye, because they have distinctive red eyes. Members of the sunfish family, rock bass are not true bass. Generally drab-colored with brown mottling over an olive body, they have the ability to change color by losing the mottling.

Their native range extends from New England across southern Canada to Manitoba and south to the Gulf States. They've also been introduced to other waters.

Though they are often larger on average than most sunfish, rock bass rarely exceed 2 pounds (0.9 kg). Two fish weighing 3 pounds (1.4 kg) are tied for the world record, one caught in Ontario's York River in 1974 and the other a 1969 catch from Indiana's Sugar Creek.

Rock bass are nest builders that spawn when water temperatures are 60 to 70°F (15.6 to 21.1°C). Males guard the nest after spawning occurs. Young rock bass grow only an inch or two (2.5 to 5.1 cm) in their first year and it may take five years or more to reach a length of 8 inches (20.3 cm).

As their name implies, they prefer rocky habitat, though you may find them in the midst of vegetation. They primarily forage near the bottom on aquatic insects and crustaceans. They do not feed much during the winter and ice anglers do not seek them.

Rock bass are less affected by changes in the weather or barometric pressure than other fish species, which means you can often catch them when other species are not biting. Typically, they struggle mightily when first hooked and then are quickly subdued. Anglers often find them in the same places where they expect to find small-mouth bass—near rocks, downed logs or trees, along weedlines, or near rocky structure. Catch one rock bass and

you are likely to catch others in the same place. In streams, look for rock bass near cover and in deeper pools, especially during the summer.

Live bait is very effective. Worms or leeches fished near the bottom produce in lakes. Stream anglers often use hellgrammites or dobsonfly larva. Small crayfish work well, too. Because they have a bigger mouth than sunfish, you can use larger hooks, generally from #8 to #4. Use a float to suspend the bait just off the bottom and avoid hang-ups. You can also tip small jigs or spinners with bait, though often it isn't necessary to entice strikes.

All small artificial lures for panfish will catch rock bass. Try casting small crankbaits, surface chuggers, spinners, or jigs with an ultralight spinning rig. You can catch rock bass throughout the day. In clear water, they may bite after dark.

■ White Perch Range

White Perch

White perch are members of the temperate bass family, which means they are related to white bass rather than yellow perch. You'll find them primarily along the Eastern Seaboard, though they have now migrated via the St. Lawrence Seaway throughout the Great Lakes. They can live in fresh, salt, and brackish waters and may migrate between saltwater estuaries and freshwater areas upstream.

Unlike white bass, they lack stripes and are generally silvery in color. Most white perch weigh 1 pound (0.5 kg) or less, though some fertile waters produce 2-pounders (0.9 kg). The world record white perch, weighing 4 pounds, 12 ounces (215 kg) came from Messalonskee Lake in Maine in 1949.

A very prolific fish, white perch are abundant wherever they are found. They spawn in tributary streams during the spring when the water temperature is between 45 and 55°F (7.2 to 12.8°C). After spawning, the adults move to ponds, estuaries, or even into the ocean.

Traveling in schools, they feed voraciously on shrimp, crabs, small fish, and insects. Generally, the schools remain in deeper water during the day and move to shallow feeding areas at night. In fall, they may migrate into tributaries to feed. Prior to the onset of winter, they retreat to big water, where they lapse into a semi-dormant state and do not feed.

One of the best times to fish for white perch is during the spring spawn, when they are concentrated in tributaries and other spawning areas. During the summer, anglers troll to locate schools of white perch in reservoirs and inland ponds. Then they cast to the school. Live bait is preferred in both situations, with worms a perennial favorite. Try various depths, because you may find the school suspended over the bottom.

You can fish them on artificial lures, with spinners getting the nod over jigs or jigging spoons. White and yellow are consistent colors for artificial lures.

Some anglers enjoy fly fishing for white perch, especially in the evening when they are actively feeding on mayflies and other insects. Dry flies and nymphs outproduce panfish poppers. Spring spawners readily strike streamers.

Although they are abundant, don't expect white perch to be pushovers. Schooling fish are skittish and may spook after you've caught a few members of the school.

Sacramento Perch

The Sacramento perch is the only native sunfish west of the Continental Divide. Originally found in the Sacramento, San Joaquin, and Pajaro drainages of California, populations declined due to habitat loss and predation by exotic fish species introduced to its native waters. Fisheries have introduced the species to waters in Nevada, Oregon, and Utah. It is able to survive in waters that are too alkaline for other fish.

It is one of the largest members of the sunfish family—the world record is a 4-pound, 9-ounce (2.06-kg) fish caught from Pyramid Lake, Nevada in 1971. The average size caught by anglers is around 1 pound (0.5 kg).

Spawning occurs in spring when the water temperature is 70°F (21.1°C). Unlike other sunfish, Sacramento perch do not make a nest or guard the spawning site, which has made them vulnerable to predation by introduced species.

Their diet consists of insects and small fish. Anglers find live minnows are the most effective bait. Fishing generally occurs during the spawning season, though you can catch them in deeper water during summer. Look for Sacramento perch near boulders and rocky cover. Work the bait slowly. You can also catch them with wet flies or nymphs fished near the bottom.

■ Sacramento Perch Range

■ Rio Grande Perch Range

Rio Grande Perch

The Rio Grande perch is an unusual and colorful fish. It is neither a perch nor a sunfish, but is a member of the cichlid family. Native to South Texas, it cannot tolerate cool water and is not found where water temperatures dip to the low 50s (10 to 15°C). Nevertheless, stocking has expanded its Texas range and it now inhabits Florida waters as well.

Similar in shape to a sunfish, the Rio Grande perch has a prominent hump on its head. A bluish-green body is speckled with bright, turquoise spots, which has led some anglers to call it the Guinea perch due to its resemblance to Guinea hen plumage.

Average weight is less than 1 pound (0.5 kg), though they occasionally top 2 pounds (0.9 kg). Spawning more than once a year, they can overpopulate small waters and become stunted.

You can raise Rio Grande perch in aquariums, though their aggressive nature makes them incompatible with other fish. This aggression can make them easy to catch. Although you can catch large Rio Grandes on small spinners or surface lures, live bait is best. Try crickets, worms, and small minnows suspended beneath a float and fished near the bottom close to aquatic vegetation. Because perch have sharp teeth, use pliers to remove hooks.

Cisco and Whitefish

Many northern lakes have substantial populations of cisco (sometimes called tullibees or herring) and lake whitefish, though they don't always attract much attention from anglers. Often this is because these fish are readily accessible to anglers only for short periods. During summer mayfly hatches, anglers take cisco. You can also catch whitefish on flies, but usually anglers are seeking walleyes or other game fish and only catch whitefish by accident. During winter, ice anglers in some locales avidly pursue whitefish and, to a lesser extent, ciscoes.

Ciscoes resemble herring; however, ciscoes are more closely related to trout and salmon than to herrings. Not surprisingly, ciscoes prefer cool and cold water and often occur in large schools that roam mid-lake areas.

Slender in body shape, they are covered with gray or silvery scales. Most weigh less than a pound (0.5 kg), though anglers occasionally catch fish weighing several pounds. The world record weighed 7 pounds, 4 ounces (3.28 kg) and came from Cedar Lake, Manitoba in 1986.

Lake whitefish are also related to trout and salmon and commonly reach larger sizes than ciscoes, averaging about 4 pounds (1.8 kg). The world record was caught in Clear Lake, Ontario in 1983 and weighed 15 pounds, 6 ounces (6.97 kg).

Although they mostly inhabit lakes, you'll also find them in large, cold rivers. As the name suggests, they are silvery-white in color. They have a small head and the mouth is located beneath a blunt snout. White-fish spawn on lake shoals or in tributary streams during the fall. They forage in shallow areas or near the surface when the water is cold, but retreat to the depths if surface temperatures become too warm during the summer.

Fly fishing for cisco and lake whitefish is probably the most popular open-water angling method. The best fishing is in May and June when mayflies hatch. Generally, they can be seen surface feeding on may-flies or other insects when the water is calm early in the morning or in the evening. Because whitefish and ciscoes cruise and feed, experienced anglers watch the rises to determine the direction that the fish is swimming and then cast ahead of it. They are slow to take the fly, so you may miss if you strike immediately on a rise. Play the fish carefully so the hook doesn't tear out of its delicate mouth. You can take whitefish on minnows or cut bait, such as a small chunk of sucker meat. They also strike jigs or jigging spoons.

Rainbow Smelt

The rainbow smelt is a small, saltwater fish that anglers introduced to lakes of the Northeast and the Great Lakes. Smelt have slender bodies with greenish backs and silvery flanks. Adults are usually 7 to 9 inches (17.8 to 22.9 cm) long. Although small, they are voracious and have a mouth lined with sharp teeth. Capture them with dip nets and seines in tributary streams or along shallow shorelines during the early spring spawning run. In winter, ice anglers capture them with hook and line.

■ Rainbow Smelt Range

Chapter 8
Ice Fishing

Across the North, a revolution has occurred on the ice. Innovations in tackle, techniques, and cold-weather gear have made ice fishing more comfortable and productive. In many locales, ice fishing for panfish is more popular than the opening-water season.

Some ice anglers even take vacations and travel to frozen lakes in other states to fish for yellow perch, crappies, and bluegills.

On the ice, you can take advantage of power augers and portable fishing shelters to stay on the move and locate active fish.

Electronic fish locators and underwater cameras let you know what is going on beneath the ice. Sophisticated rods and tackle allow you to fine-tune fishing presentations.

The revolution has made ice anglers more effective than ever before. And ice fishing has never been so fun!

Ice Fishing Shelters

Ice anglers once relied on plywood shanties to stay out of the elements and keep warm while fishing. Ranging from simple shelters to elaborate structures that may include everything from bunk beds to all the comforts of home (including television), shanties are a great way to beat the cold and snow. They do have one drawback—a lack of mobility. Once you set up a shanty, you are unlikely to move it until the season's end. Pick a good

location and you'll likely catch fish. But you won't catch as many as an angler who can move about on the ice. When ice fishing, you are limited to just the small area beneath the hole you've drilled in the ice. There may be only a few active fish in the vicinity. An angler on the move can keep seeking active fish.

Available in many different makes and models, you can quickly and easily carry or tow a portable shelter out onto the ice in a likely spot. You can fish comfortably and, if the fish aren't biting, move to another spot. You can also use a portable shelter as a temporary base of operations and drill more holes in its vicinity. Then you can move from one hole to another seeking active fish and retreat to your shelter if you get cold and need to warm up.

Most portable shelters are built with a sled or runner system so they slide easily across the ice. Some are small enough for you to pull by hand. Others, built for more than one person, need a snowmobile or all-terrain vehicle to tow it. Some have storage compartments for your gear and built-in seating. Most have a floor with openings for your fishing holes.

When selecting a portable shelter, be sure that it breaks down to a size that will fit in your vehicle for transporting to and from the lake.

Portable shelters provide maximum flexibility and come in a wide variety of sizes.

Electronics

Sophisticated electronics have aided the ice-fishing revolution. Many panfish anglers consider a fish finder to be an essential ice-fishing tool. Some fish finders have a liquid crystal display that gives a chart read-out, showing the bottom and marks representing fish. Most ice anglers prefer flasher units because they are more sensitive and easier to read when ice fishing. Using a flasher, you can see your bait on the screen, as well as see any fish. Pay careful attention to your flasher and you can even watch fish swim up to investigate your bait. Then you get ready for the bite! Flashers designed for ice fishing come in carrying cases and have mounts that allow you to set up the transducer in your fishing hole.

Another popular fishing aid is the underwater camera. You can lower the camera unit on a cable to any depth and you'll see the video images displayed on a small screen. You can turn the camera 360 degrees to survey the area. The camera is helpful for identifying fish species and you can use it to monitor your bait.

Unfortunately, you can also see the big one that gets away.

On large bodies of water, anglers use Global Positioning Systems (GPS) to mark fishing locations. You'll often find crappies, yellow perch, and bluegills in locations that are difficult to locate with a shoreline landmark. Entering the position on a GPS unit allows you to find the place again with excellent accuracy. You can store locations in the unit's memory and find them again from one year to the next. Some lake contour maps even include the GPS coordinates of popular fishing locations.

Gear

You need some special equipment to fish through the ice. First and foremost is an auger or a chisel to cut a fishing hole. A chisel is adequate for cutting a hole through a few inches of ice or for re-opening a frozen fishing hole. A sharp hand auger will quickly cut through thick ice, provided you are in decent physical condition. Small-diameter hand augers—6 inches (15.2 cm) or less—are the easiest to use.

An auger powered with a gasoline engine is the most efficient way to cut holes, though some anglers believe the noise and vibrations associated with these machines may spook wary fish. If the noise may be a problem where you fish, use the auger a half hour or more before you expect the prime-time bite to begin. You can buy augers that will cut holes anywhere from 4 to 12 inches (10.2 to 30.5 cm) in diameter.

Although many anglers enjoy fishing through them, large-diameter holes often aren't necessary for panfish. Be aware, too, that unsuspecting anglers and children may step into a larger hole. Doing so usually isn't life threatening, but plunging thigh deep into cold water can quickly ruin an otherwise pleasant day.

Whatever tool you choose to cut through the ice, be sure it is sharp. A dull blade can make cutting holes a tedious task. Keep the blades covered with a guard when not in use to prevent accidents.

Other ice-fishing essentials include a skimmer to clear ice chips from your holes. A 5-gallon (19-l) bucket can serve as a tackle box and a handy seat. Stow your gear on a lightweight toboggan or in a rucksack.

Even if the day is warm, dress in layers (you can always remove heavy clothes) and wear gloves or mittens. In fact, experienced anglers often bring a spare pair of mittens or choppers in case the first pair gets wet. Bring a towel to dry your hands. Pocket hand-warmers are helpful, too. Always wear warm headgear. Insulated, waterproof boots will keep you comfortable when standing on ice or sloshing through slush. Your body requires extra energy to stay warm during cold weather, so it is always a good idea to bring along something to eat and drink.

Ice
skimmer

Modern shelters have many convenient amenities, and are much like a home away from home.

Drill a hole with a power auger (in use), hand auger (middle) or Swedish cup-style drill (right). Some augers have handle extensions for extra thick ice.

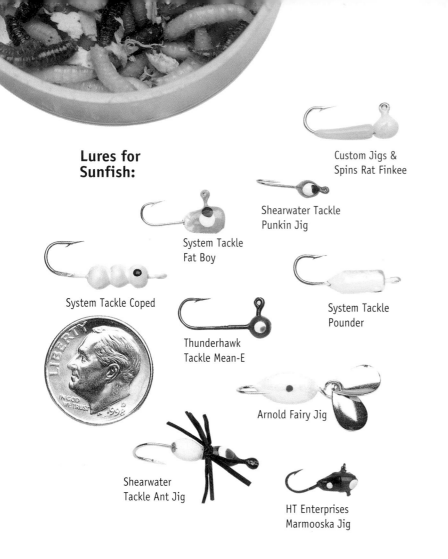

Lures for Sunfish:

Custom Jigs & Spins Rat Finkee

Shearwater Tackle Punkin Jig

System Tackle Fat Boy

System Tackle Coped

System Tackle Pounder

Thunderhawk Tackle Mean-E

Arnold Fairy Jig

Shearwater Tackle Ant Jig

HT Enterprises Marmooska Jig

Tackle

An array of tackle designed for panfish situations is available, including rods, reels, lines, and lures. Choosing the proper tackle to meet your needs can be a daunting task, though one that can be made considerably easier by seeking help at a fishing shop. In general, avoid bargain, "all in one" setups. Select a rod that is sensitive, but has enough backbone to set the hook and play fish of the size you intend to catch. If you are fishing for bluegill or crappie, use line from 1- to 4-pound-test (0.5- to 1.8-kg), so your rod must be limber enough to accommodate light line. Spool the line on a small spinning reel with a smooth drag. For yellow perch, whitefish, and cisco you can use medium-light to medium rods and reels, because you may use larger lures and baits. It is unlikely you will need to use line heavier than 6-pound-test (2.7-kg).

The importance of using light, thin-diameter lines for ice fishing cannot be overstated. In the winter, most lakes have very clear water, so fishing lines are more visible to the fish. Light lines sink more easily with the tiny baits typically used for panfish. In a vertical, ice-fishing presentation, using a light line makes it easier to impart action to the bait with minimal movements.

Some manufacturers offer lines especially designed for ice fishing that resist water absorption and are less likely to freeze, but any quality, low-visibility line will suffice. Change your fishing line at the beginning of every winter season and more often if you frequently go ice fishing.

The lures used for ice fishing come in endless styles and colors, but share a common trait: All are designed for vertical fishing presentations. Be sure you know the proper action for any lure you intend to use. Some wiggle enticingly. Others jig and hop. Still others dart or glide from side to side. How well you impart the proper action to the lure will, in part, determine your fishing success.

Color is another important factor when selecting ice-fishing lures. Hot or bright colors are often preferred for their attractor qualities. Glow gets the nod for night, low-light, or dark-water fishing conditions. Carry a selection of lures in various colors to prepare you for a variety of fishing situations.

In some places, it is legal to use two or more lines when fishing through the ice. You can drill two fishing holes side by side, then use an active presentation in one while still-fishing bait beneath a float in the other. Sometimes, fish attracted by your active presentation strike the other bait.

You can also use a tip-up to place a bait some distance away from where you are actively fishing. When a fish strikes the bait, it trips a flag or similar indicator so you know you have a bite. Tip-ups are most effective when fishing for aggressive feeders such as yellow perch.

Lures for Crappies:

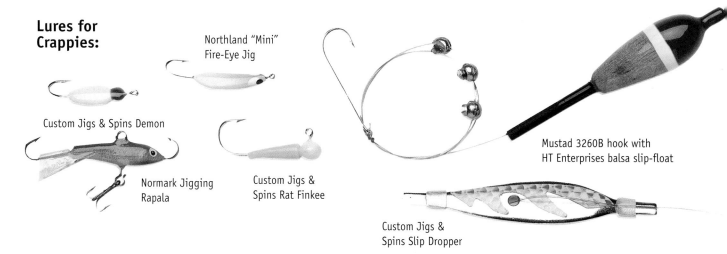

Northland "Mini" Fire-Eye Jig

Custom Jigs & Spins Demon

Normark Jigging Rapala

Custom Jigs & Spins Rat Finkee

Mustad 3260B hook with HT Enterprises balsa slip-float

Custom Jigs & Spins Slip Dropper

Lures for Yellow Perch:

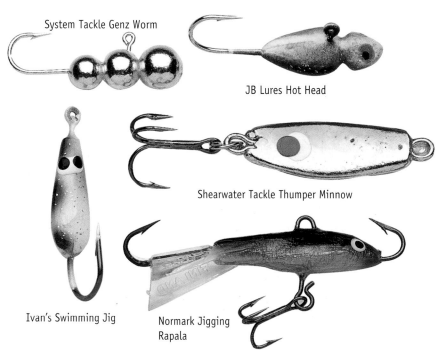

System Tackle Genz Worm

JB Lures Hot Head

Shearwater Tackle Thumper Minnow

Ivan's Swimming Jig

Normark Jigging Rapala

Safety

Whenever you venture out on a frozen waterway, safety comes first. The best ice fishing often occurs at first and last ice, when conditions are the most unpredictable. Currents, snow melt, and the rate of freezing can cause ice thickness to vary considerably—safe ice may be just a few steps away from dangerously thin ice. If you are unsure of the conditions, avoid inlets and outlets, aeration systems, current areas, and patches of open water.

Very large water bodies may form heaves and pressure ridges, where the pressure of expanding ice (water expands when it freezes) causes it to crack, break, and heave. Open water can occur along the break line and snow may cover it. Be very careful when crossing such areas; avoid them if possible.

On the Great Lakes, wind and wave action may create pack ice when an ice sheet breaks up, moves, piles up, and refreezes. Anglers who fish in situations where wind and waves may move the ice often skid a small boat or canoe across the ice so they can cross open leads and return to shore.

Veteran anglers are always cautious on the ice. Some carry ice spikes to pull themselves back up onto the ice if they break through. Others test the ice ahead with hard pokes from a chisel as they walk. Early-season ice, uncovered by snow, may be slick and make for difficult walking. You can strap a pair of ice creepers onto the soles of your boots for traction. Ice-fishing with a buddy is always a good idea. And make sure someone knows where you plan to fish.

In the North, driving on frozen waterways with all-terrain vehicles, snowmobiles, cars, and trucks is common. However, drivers occasionally break through the ice. Be forewarned that your insurance company is unlikely to cover the damages. If you choose to drive on the ice, stick to well-traveled areas.

Cold weather requires additional safety considerations, too. If you fish from a heated shelter, be sure the heater is safe. Carbon monoxide poisoning is a danger. Use a heater that is intended for use in a confined space.

Always dress for winter conditions. Wear felt-insulated boots and two pairs of socks. Dress in layers of clothing and be sure the outer layer is waterproof. You can count on water splashing you when drilling holes; the ice may be flooded with several inches of water or slush. Avoid cotton clothing, because it retains moisture and can chill you. If you begin shivering and become uncomfortably cold, do what it takes to get warm—including packing up and heading off the lake. Hypothermia can be a killer.

Ice cleats

Ice picks

Test ice of uncertain thickness by whacking it with a sharp chisel. If the chisel breaks through or the ice cracks, trace your path back to shore.

The pressure of expanding ice causes it to crack and heave, sometimes forming pockets of open water between the chunks.

Spring Bobber Savvy

Winter panfish are light-biters and detecting strikes is the greatest challenge to icing big bluegills or crappies. You may not feel a tap on a jiggle stick or notice any movement with a float when a slab inhales and then quickly exhales the bait. The best way to detect these sneaky strikes is with a spring bobber, the most sensitive strike indicator.

Made of fine steel or a similar material, the spring bobber extends beyond the rod tip and has an eye for the line to pass through. Far more sensitive than even the most limber ice rod, a spring bobber instantly telegraphs the faintest movements of your bait. Since winter panfish are notorious for soft strikes, savvy anglers say that using a spring bobber will significantly increase your catch.

If you observe panfish approaching a bait with an underwater camera or by looking down a fishing hole, you'll notice the big ones are invariably light biters. They glide up beside the bait, pause, then suck it in without changing their position. The bait barely moves. Catching these cautious fish requires finesse.

Serious panfish practitioners use remarkably small and light tackle. Standard medicine for light-biters is 1-pound-test (0.5 kg) line rigged with a #14 ice lure tipped with a larva—a setup effective for both bluegills and crappies. If you are after slab crappies, which may weigh more than 1 pound (0.5 kg), step up to 2-pound-test (0.9-kg) and a #12 ice lure.

When fishing with a spring bobber, you may expect it to dip into a deep bend when you get a bite, but that doesn't happen often with big panfish, especially bluegills. Usually, all you'll notice is a slight twitch as a fish takes the bait. You must watch closely to see faint bobber movements when fishing with small baits. You can use a bead or bright paint on the spring bobber to make strikes easier to see.

Tiny baits are best for panfish, because scuds and aquatic insects are their primary winter food sources. When using light lines and baits, make sure your technique is as delicate as the tackle. Don't add a split shot so that a #14 ice lure sinks more quickly, because it will destroy the action. The small-diameter, 1- or 2-pound-test (0.5- to 0.9-kg) line allows it to descend at a reasonable rate, and panfish often take a slowly free-falling bait as it enters their zone.

Likewise, don't overwork the bait with an overactive jig or jiggle. Instead, turn your fishing rod so you can reach the rod tip with your free hand. Then use your forefinger to lightly tap the spring bobber. Your tiny bait will dance with enticing motion.

Try fishing an ascending bait at various levels, beginning near the bottom. Quickly raise the bait about 10 inches (25.4 cm) with an arm movement, allow it to remain stationary, and then lift again. The ascending movement imitates the natural motion of scuds, a favorite winter food source.

You can use a flasher to locate fish, but don't expect to use it to detect strikes. Remember, if you wait to feel a tug or tap, the fish is feeling resistance, too. With a well-tuned spring bobber, there is no resistance. Adjust the length of a spring bobber by moving it along the rod tip. The farther the spring bobber extends, the more sensitive it is to line movements. A good rule of thumb is that a properly adjusted spring bobber should bend at about a 30-degree angle from the rod from the weight of your line and bait.

Sometimes, when the fish are especially finicky, you can make a kink in the line just below the bobber so you can see the slightest line movement. In any case, when you see the bobber or the line move, immediately set the hook. When a spring bobber twitches, you can be confident the fish has the bait.

Pumpkinseed and bluegill (top and bottom) are often fished at the same time.

Bluegill Tactics

Ice fishing for bluegills is fun and productive. If you know where to find them, bluegills often remain active throughout the winter, though the best action is at first ice and just before ice-out. At first ice, look for bluegills in vegetation or along its outer edge, usually in water less than 10 feet (3.0 m) deep. As the vegetation decays during the winter, it uses up oxygen, causing the fish to move to deeper water. On most lakes, sunfish wintering areas are well known, so you can find them by looking for other anglers. Otherwise, try depths up to 25 feet (7.6 m) in areas near vegetation.

Sunfish are usually near the bottom. Although they are often willing to bite, a finesse presentation will put more fish on the ice. Use very light line and tiny teardrops, ice flies, jigs, and similar lures tipped with a grub, mousie, or waxworm.

Movement attracts bluegills, but too much movement will work against you. Just jiggle or shake the rod to make your bait quiver, jiggle, and twitch. Pause frequently. Often bluegills will approach to inspect a moving bait, but only bite when the movement stops. Use a spring bobber to detect the light strikes.

Winter bluegills may not move very far to go after your bait. When you begin fishing, auger several holes in the same vicinity. If you are not getting action at the first hole, try another one. Some veteran anglers recommend moving frequently, as often as every five minutes if you are not getting bites.

Use your electronic flasher to look for fish that are approaching your bait but not striking. Similar-size sunfish school together. If you are catching small fish, try moving to adjacent deeper water to find bigger ones.

Crappie Tactics

Crappies are a reliable standby for ice anglers. They remain active throughout the winter, though fishing is best just after the ice forms and again in late winter. Crappie schools are mobile, but the schools return to the same locations, which are where anglers place their fishing shanties.

Look for crappies near vegetation, off points or drop-offs, and along the edge of structure. Active crappies often move into these locations early in the morning or late in the day. They also bite well at night.

Winter crappies may suspend anywhere from the bottom to just beneath the ice. A good starting point to try for suspended crappies is two-thirds of the way to the bottom.

Crappies are easy to see on electronic flashers, which many anglers consider essential equipment. If you are not having any action, try drilling a few more holes and remember to move around. Sometimes schooling crappies are nearby. It is not uncommon for an angler to have a "hot hole" while others in the vicinity are catching few fish.

Small minnows fished on a plain hook or with a jigging lure are the most common winter crappie baits. However, some anglers believe that a sunfish setup—larvae fished on tiny ice lures—is more effective and accounts for bigger crappies. When the fish are finicky, the tiny, finesse presentations may trigger more strikes. You can also use commercial scents or bait products.

When you catch a crappie, pay careful attention to the depth you are fishing. Very likely, you will catch another fish at the same depth. Since crappies travel in schools, it is not unusual to have a flurry of fishing activity. Quickly rebait and get your line back in the water after catching a fish. When crappies are active, unbaited jigging lures may be as productive as the real thing.

If you are using a minnow, you can suspend the bait with a tiny float. Choose a style that offers little resistance when a fish bites and a size that is just big enough to remain afloat when suspending your bait.

When you get a bite, the bobber may twitch or pop beneath the surface several times before it begins to submerge. When it goes down, pick up your line until it is tight and then lift to set the hook. As always, play a crappie carefully to prevent the hook from tearing free.

Keep a good bend in the rod while fighting crappies, or for that matter, any species of fish. If you give crappies slack line, the hook may slip out.

Yellow Perch Tactics

In northern regions, yellow perch have a fanatical following among ice anglers. The species is so popular that ice fishing for perch boosts winter tourism in some locales. Fish management agencies have reduced perch bag limits on many lakes to protect the prolific fish from overharvest.

The popularity of yellow perch can be attributed to two things. One is the fact they are abundant and ready biters during the winter. The second, more important, reason is they are so good to eat. In many places, perch filets are the main ingredient in Friday-night fish fries.

Since perch are fairly easy to catch, ice-fishing tactics are relatively unsophisticated. The real trick is locating larger perch, typically females, which anglers call jumbos or cows in various locales. Jumbos are at least 9 inches (22.9 cm) long and may weigh upwards of 1 pound (0.5 kg).

The best jumbo action is usually in late winter, peaking just before ice-out, when perch move into waters less than 10 feet (3.0 m) deep to feed prior to the spring spawn. At that time, look for them along shallow flats or near rock piles. Earlier in the winter, look for them in deeper water along the edges of sand and mud flats, near breaklines, or on the deep side of a drop-off.

You can catch perch throughout the day and in a variety of weather conditions. During a tough bite, try fishing early in the morning.

Anglers commonly use minnows for bait, though in some regions anglers prefer to use perch eyes. You can hook a live minnow on a #6 or #4 hook and suspend it beneath a float.

Many anglers prefer using jigs. The jigging action may draw more strikes than still-fishing with a live minnow. In a tough bite, tip a small jig with a minnow head. You can use mayfly nymphs, larvae, angleworms, and even marshmallows as bait.

Whitefish and Cisco Tactics

Many northern lakes support abundant populations of whitefish and cisco. These cold-water species remain active through the winter months, though their popularity with anglers varies from region to region. Often anglers pursue them in late winter, after the fishing seasons for game species have closed.

Both whitefish and cisco have firm, white flesh, but they do not keep well when frozen. Most folks prefer to eat them fresh, smoked, or pickled.

Lake whitefish are large, frequently weighing from 2 to 6 pounds (0.9 to 2.7 kg). A smaller whitefish, the menomonie, is found in the Great Lakes. Cisco typically weigh less than one pound. All species have small, delicate mouths.

Fishing typically occurs in areas with moderate or deep water. Use jigging spoons or jigs for whitefish, perhaps tipped with a minnow head or an entire minnow. Still-fishing with a live minnow on a plain hook can be effective. To locate whitefish, begin fishing near the bottom and use an electronic fish finder to find active fish.

For cisco, you could try bluegill gear, especially small flies and lures tipped with larva. Fast action usually occurs when you locate a school of hungry fish, which may be suspended at any depth—even just beneath the ice.

Whitefish (top). **Cisco** (bottom).

White Bass Tactics

Although many waters that contain white bass do not freeze over, some ice fishing occurs in the northern part of their range. Look for them in the same locations where you find them during the summer, though they may be somewhat deeper. Due to their roving nature, they may be difficult to locate. Keep drilling holes and moving until you find them.

To fish quickly and draw strikes, use jigging lures. You can tip the jig with a minnow, though usually it isn't necessary to do so. Focus your fishing efforts near the bottom. Use somewhat heavier tackle than you would for crappies. A medium-action jigging stick rigged with a spinning reel spooled with 6- to 8-pound-test (2.7- to 3.6-kg) line is a good choice.

Smelt Tactics

Ice fishing for smelt occurs from New England to the Great Lakes, though its popularity is often localized. Smelt are small, saltwater bait fish ranging from 6 to 9 inches (15.2 to 22.9 cm) in length that have been widely introduced in cold northern waters as a forage species. Some ice anglers catch them to use as bait for game fish, while others enjoy eating fried smelt.

In winter, smelt often suspend at depths of 25 to 75 feet (7.6 to 22.9 m). As spring approaches, they gather off the mouths of tributaries in preparation for the spawning run that occurs shortly after ice-out.

Along the East Coast, you'll find them in frozen estuaries, where they hold in large eddies. In many waters, smelt bite best at night.

Use larvae, minnows, or sea worms (on the East Coast) for bait. Tiny, #10 or #12 hooks are necessary. Where allowed, you can use multiple-hook rigs to catch more than one smelt at a time. In some locales, anglers use special speed reels to quickly raise and lower their line from deep water. In most situations, bluegill gear will suffice.

Chapter 9
Eating Your Catch

For most anglers, the point of angling for panfish is to catch dinner. Nearly all panfish have mild-flavored, white flesh that can be prepared in many ways. In fact, the various panfish species are the most abundant and popular freshwater food fish in North America.

Panfish Asparagus Biscuit Bake

1 cup (240 ml) diced carrot
1 small onion, chopped
2 tablespoons (30 g) margarine or butter
2 cups (480 ml) flaked cooked panfish or other lean fish
1 can (10¾ ounces/304 g) condensed cream of mushroom soup
1 package (10 ounces/283 g) frozen asparagus cuts, thawed
½ cup (120 ml) milk, divided
2 teaspoons (10 ml) fresh lemon juice
¼ teaspoon (1.25 ml) salt
⅛ teaspoon (0.6 ml) pepper
1 cup (240 ml) buttermilk baking mix
1 teaspoon (5 ml) dried parsley flakes
Dash paprika

4 to 6 servings

Heat oven to 375°F (174°C). In 9-inch (23 cm) skillet, cook and stir carrot and onion in margarine over medium heat until tender, about 11 minutes. Remove to 1½-quart (1.4 liter) casserole. Stir in fish, cream of mushroom soup, asparagus cuts, ¼ cup (60 ml) milk, lemon juice, salt, and pepper. Set aside.

In small bowl, combine baking mix, ⅓ cup (80 ml) milk, parsley flakes and paprika. Mix with fork. Drop eight mounds of dough on fish mixture in casserole.

Bake until biscuits are golden brown and casserole is bubbly, about 35 minutes. Brush biscuits with melted margarine before serving, if desired.

Fishing for panfish is most popular during the cool seasons—spring, winter, and autumn—because this is often when the fish bite best. Many anglers also believe that panfish caught from cool water have firmer flesh, better flavor, and fewer parasites. The latter is not necessarily true, because panfish can carry parasites throughout the year. Panfish parasites are fairly common, but are harmless to humans if the flesh is thoroughly cooked.

Lemon Fried Panfish

1 cup (240 ml) all-purpose flour
2 teaspoons (10 ml) grated lemon peel
½ teaspoon (2.5 ml) salt
¼ teaspoon (2.5 ml) pepper
1 cup (240 ml) water
Vegetable oil
1½ pounds (680 g) panfish fillets
All-purpose flour

4 to 6 servings

In medium bowl, combine flour, lemon peel, salt, and pepper. Blend in water; cover. Refrigerate at least 30 minutes.

In deep-fat fryer or deep skillet, heat oil (1½ to 3 inches/3.8 to 7.6 cm) to 375°F (174°C). Coat fish with flour, then dip in chilled batter. Fry a few pieces at a time, turning occasionally, until light golden brown, about 3 minutes. Drain on paper towels. Keep warm in 175°F (79°C) oven. Repeat with remaining fish.

Hearty Vegetable and Panfish Soup

4 slices bacon, cut up
1 medium onion, chopped
1 small green pepper, chopped
¼ cup (60 ml) chopped celery
1 clove garlic, minced
4 tomatoes, peeled and chopped
2 cups (470 ml) sliced fresh mushrooms
2 cups (470 ml) water
1 can (6 ounces/175 ml) tomato paste
½ cup (125 ml) white wine
1 tablespoon plus 1 teaspoon (15 ml)
   instant chicken bouillon granules
1 bay leaf
½ teaspoon (2.5 ml) dried oregano leaves
½ teaspoon (2.5 ml)sugar
¼ teaspoon (1.25 ml)ground sage
1 pound (454 g) panfish fillets

4 to 6 servings

In Dutch oven, cook bacon over medium-high heat, stirring occasionally, until crisp. Remove with slotted spoon; set aside. Add onion, green pepper, celery, and garlic. Cook and stir over medium heat until vegetables are tender, 6 to 7 minutes. Add bacon and remaining ingredients except fish. Simmer, stirring occasionally, for 30 minutes. Cut fillets into 1-inch (2.5 cm) pieces. Add to soup. Simmer, stirring gently, until fish flakes easily, about 8 minutes.

Creamy Tomato and Panfish Soup

2 large red potatoes (about 1 pound/454 g)
1 medium onion, chopped
¼ cup (60 ml) chopped celery
3 tablespoons (45 g) margarine or butter
2¼ cups (270 ml) cold water, divided
1 can (16 ounces/450 ml) whole tomatoes, drained

½ cup (125 ml) white wine
1 teaspoon (5 ml) salt
Dash pepper
3 tablespoons (50 ml) all-purpose flour
½ cup (60 ml) half-and-half
1 pound (454 g) panfish fillets

4 to 6 servings

Peel potatoes; cut into ¼-inch (6 mm) cubes. Set aside. In 3-quart (2.8 liter) saucepan, cook and stir onion and celery in margarine over medium heat until tender-crisp, about 5 minutes. Add potato cubes, 2 cups (240 ml) water, tomatoes, wine, salt, and pepper. Blend flour into ¼ cup (30 ml) water; stir into vegetable mixture. Heat to boiling. Reduce heat. Cover and simmer, stirring occasionally, until potatoes are tender, 20 minutes. Stir in half-and-half. Cut fillets into 1-inch (2.5 cm) pieces. Add to soup. Cover and simmer, stirring gently one or two times, until fish flakes easily, about 8 minutes.

Panfish Chowder

6 slices bacon, cut up
3 medium red potatoes (1 pound/454 g)
⅔ cup (160 ml) chopped onion
½ cup (60 ml) chopped celery
2 cups (240 ml) fish stock*
1 cup (240 ml) sliced fresh mushrooms
½ cup (60 ml) chopped carrot
¼ cup (30 ml) snipped fresh parsley

1 tablespoon (10 ml) fresh lemon or lime juice
1 teaspoon (5 ml) salt
½ teaspoon (2.5 ml) dried dillweed
⅛ teaspoon (0.6 ml) dried fennel seed
⅛ teaspoon (0.6 ml) garlic salt
⅛ teaspoon 0.6 ml) pepper
1 cup (240 ml)p half-and-half
1½ cups (350 ml) cut-up cooked panfish (about 1½-inch (3.8 cm) pieces)

4 to 6 servings

In 3-quart (2.8 liter) saucepan, cook bacon over medium-high heat, stirring occasionally, until crisp. Remove with slotted spoon; set aside. Peel potatoes and cut into ¼-inch (6 mm) cubes; set aside.

Cook and stir onion and celery in bacon fat over medium-high heat until tender, about 5 minutes. Add bacon, potato cubes, fish stock, mushrooms, carrot, parsley, lemon juice, salt, dillweed, fennel seed, garlic salt, and pepper. Heat to boiling. Reduce heat. Cover and simmer until vegetables are tender, 15 to 20 minutes. Blend in half-and-half. Gently stir in fish pieces. Skim fat, if desired.

*Or, substitute 2 cups (480 ml) water and 2 teaspoons (10 ml) instant chicken bouillon granules; omit the salt.

Afterword
Panfish Conservation

Panfish were once considered a resource of nearly limitless abundance and were regulated with continuous open seasons and high bag limits. Unfortunately, increased fishing pressure and, in some instances, habitat loss have taken a toll on panfish populations in many waters. In such situations, the fish remain abundant, but their average size decreases. As the jumbos and slabs become less numerous, angler satisfaction diminishes. It is hard to get excited about fishing for panfish when most of the fish you catch are too small to keep and eat. Fish managers are then faced with a difficult task—they must find a way to increase the size of panfish and satisfy anglers.

Often, the only way to boost the numbers of larger fish in the population is to reduce the harvest or increase the number of panfish predators. The problem is that either strategy is likely to adversely affect someone's fishing. Anglers may complain about catching runts but nevertheless be reluctant to accept reduced bag limits, particularly when they are accustomed to taking home fish by the bucketful and are now told they may take only a few.

Even when the size structure in the population improves, fish managers are reluctant to adopt more generous limits, because overfishing may again occur. As a result, anglers must adjust to lower bag limits at some popular fishing holes.

Habitat loss and non-point-source pollution are more insidious and no quick, easy, or inexpensive fix can remedy the problem. In some instances, runoff from fertilized lawns and farm fields, sediments from erosion, and other pollution sources reduce water quality. Chemical contaminants in the water or in the food chain may accumulate in fish and make them unsafe to eat. Shoreline development, aquatic plant removal, artificially controlled water levels, and dredging or other waterway alterations can limit or eliminate spawning and nursery habitat. As habitat disappears, fish populations decline—a sad reality occurring in many waterways.

What can anglers do to protect or improve their fishing? First and foremost, practice conservation when you fish by keeping only as many fish as you need. Even when they are abundant, panfish are not an inexhaustible resource. Second, learn about the forms of pollution and habitat degradation that are likely to affect the waters where you

fish, then find a way to get involved in conservation efforts. It may be as simple as joining a local fishing club and participating in their conservation projects. Or it may require the commitment necessary to be appointed to a local planning or zoning board. Sometimes, protecting your favorite fishing spots may require writing letters to your elected representatives.

Occasionally, you can even make a difference for fishing at the ballot box. Whatever pathway you choose, the important thing to remember is that fishing provides you many pleasurable experiences. Devoting time and energy to fish conservation is one way for you to give something back. Your contribution to conservation is an investment in the future of angling.

Index

Contributing Photographers

Mark Emery
Ocala, Florida
© Mark Emery: pp. 32, 35 (bottom), 71

Eric Engbretson
Florence, Wisconsin
© Eric Engbretson/underwaterfish-photos.com: pp. 27, 28, 33 (left), 38, 45, 46, 61, 62, 63, 81

Bill Lindner
Minneapolis, MN
© Bill Lindner Photography/blpstudio.com: pp. 6, 9, 18, 19, 20, 25 (top), 57, 86, 89, 90, 93 (top), front cover

Tom Migdalski
Hamden, Connecticut
© Tom Migdalski: pp. 25 (bottom), 55

Doug Stamm
Sauk City, Wisconsin
© Doug Stamm/stammphoto.com: pp. 3 (all), 4, 7, 8, 10, 26, 29, 30, 31, 33 (right), 47, 70, 82, 83, 91, 99, back cover (top)

Creative Publishing international
Your Complete Source of How-to Information for the Outdoors

The Complete
FLY FISHERMAN™